Sustainability

Project Book

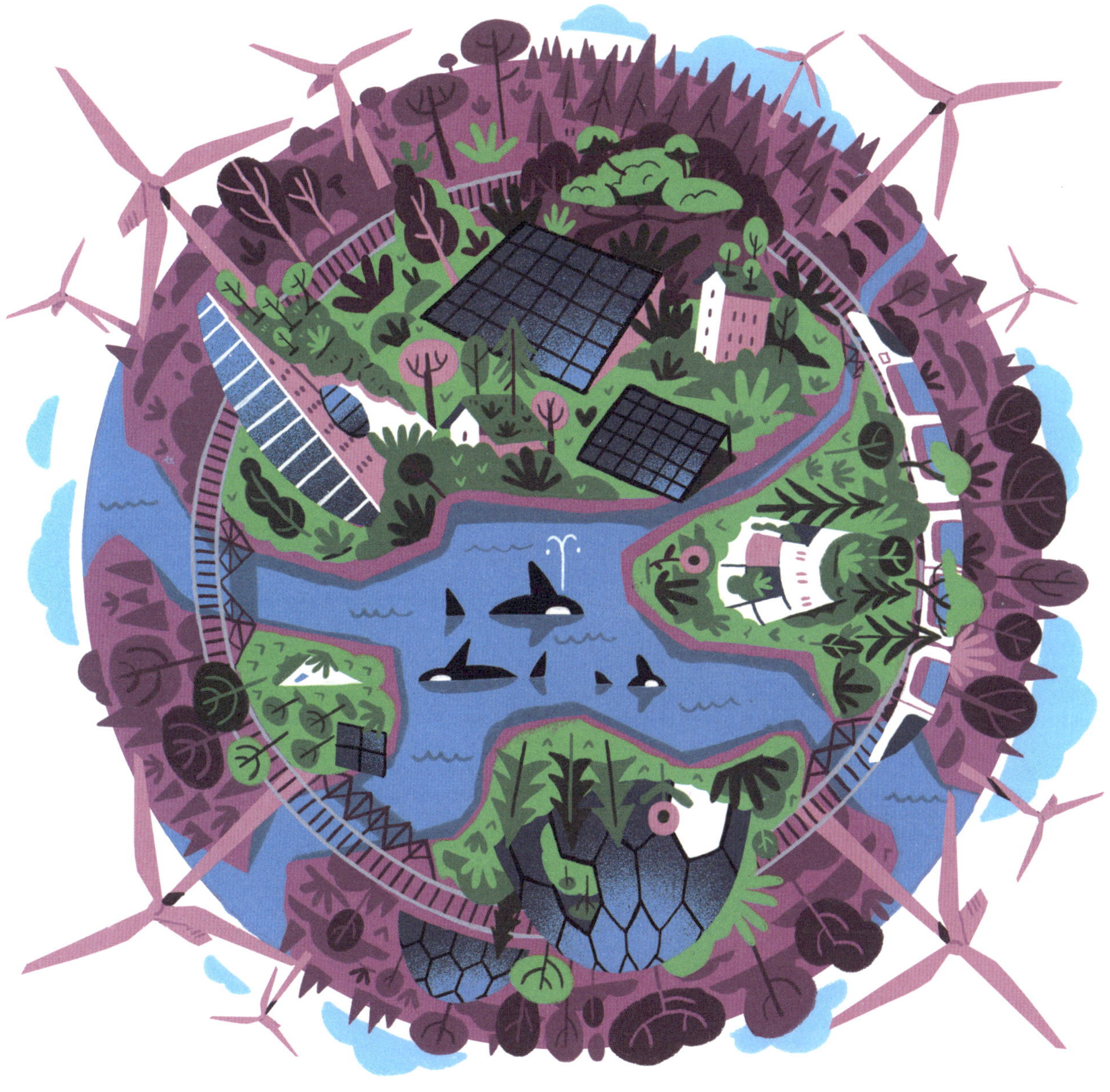

Rebecca Tudor

OXFORD

Great Clarendon Street, Oxford, OX2 6DP, United Kingdom

Oxford University Press is a department of the University of Oxford. It furthers the University's objective of excellence in research, scholarship, and education by publishing worldwide. Oxford is a registered trade mark of Oxford University Press in the UK and in certain other countries

British Library Cataloguing in Publication Data
Data available

978-1-38-204750-0

10 9 8 7 6 5 4 3 2 1

The manufacturing process conforms to the environmental regulations of the country of origin.

Printed in India by Multivista Global Pvt. Ltd.

Acknowledgements

The publisher and author would like to thank the following for permission to use photographs and other copyright material:

Artwork: Cover artwork by Gerhard van Wyk. All other artwork by Peters & Zabransky, Angela Knowles, Stéphan Theron, Aptara Inc, and Q2A Media. **Photos: p7:** Alessandro D'Esposito/Shutterstock; **p8 (t, l):** Indian Food Images/Shutterstock; **p8 (t, r):** nikkimeel/Shutterstock; **p8 (b, l):** Smileus/Shutterstock; **p8 (b, r):** xamnesiacx84/Shutterstock; **p10 (t, l):** Larina Marina/Shutterstock; **p10 (t, r):** oticki/Shutterstock; **p10 (b):** Carolina Jaramillo/Shutterstock; **p12 (t, l):** NadyGinzburg/Shutterstock; **p12 (t, r):** Morten B/Shutterstock; **p12 (b):** Tara Lambourne/Shutterstock; **p14 (m):** Jazzmany/Shutterstock; **p14 (1):** monticello/Shutterstock; **p14 (2):** Africa Studio/Shutterstock; **p14 (3):** dilyaz/Shutterstock; **p14 (4):** Nopparat Promtha/Shutterstock; **p14 (5):** Ground Picture/Shutterstock; **p14 (6):** Drazen Zigic/Shutterstock; **p15:** Peter Wollinga/Shutterstock; **p16 (t, l):** Cast Of Thousands/Shutterstock; **p16 (t, r):** Frank11/Shutterstock; **p16 (b):** Anton_Ivanov/Shutterstock; **p17 (l):** Vecton/Shutterstock; **p17 (t, r):** Kirana J/Shutterstock; **p17 (b, r):** gnomeandi/Shutterstock; **p18 (t, l):** Jinning Li/Shutterstock; **p18 (t, r):** kamilpetran/Shutterstock; **p18 (b):** Tinnakorn jorruang/Shutterstock; **p19:** Elnur/Shutterstock; **p20 (t):** macri roland/Shutterstock; **p20 (m):** Sueddeutsche Zeitung Photo/Alamy Stock Photo; **p20 (b):** Associated Press/Alamy Stock Photo; **p21 (t, l):** YAKOBCHUK VIACHESLAV/Shutterstock; **p21 (t, r):** Moh. Saefudin/Shutterstock; **p21 (b):** Rawpixel.com/Shutterstock; **p23 (t, l):** Ink Drop/Shutterstock; **p23 (t, r):** TK Kurikawa/Shutterstock; **p23 (b):** DOERS/Shutterstock; **p24 (b):** Roop_Dey/Shutterstock; **p24 (t, r):** PeopleImages.com - Yuri A/Shutterstock; **p24 (m, r):** New Africa/Shutterstock; **p24 (t, l):** GeorgesDaya/Shutterstock; **p24 (m, l):** Tarek Islam/Shutterstock; **p25 (t, l):** woraatep suppavas/Shutterstock; **p25 (b):** Sunshine Seeds/Shutterstock; **p25 (t, r):** Warren Parker/Shutterstock; **p27:** Koto Amatsukami/Shutterstock; **p30 (t, l):** Anastasiia Lozynska/Shutterstock; **p30 (t, r):** fabiano goreme caddeo/Shutterstock; **p30 (b, l):** hanahusain/Shutterstock; **p30 (b, r):** Olga Kashubin/Shutterstock; **p34 (l):** FocusStocker/Shutterstock; **p34 (r):** Zdenek Sasek/Shutterstock; **p35 (t, l):** R.Suresh Babu/Shutterstock; **p35 (t, r):** Sergii Figurnyi/Shutterstock; **p35 (b, r):** Patrick Foto/Shutterstock; **p35 (b, l):** ChameleonsEye/Shutterstock; **p37 (l):** Margy Crane/Shutterstock; **p37 (r):** FeriDhaniHasri/Shutterstock; **p40 (t, l):** monticello/Shutterstock; **p40 (t, r):** Jne Valokuvaus/Shutterstock; **p40 (b, r):** cowardlion/Shutterstock; **p40 (b, l):** Rawpixel.com/Shutterstock; **p41 (l):** TommyStockProject/Shutterstock; **p41 (m):** Chachamp/Shutterstock; **p41 (r):** Sergey Hramov/Shutterstock; **p42 (l):** Alison Hancock/Shutterstock; **p42 (r):** dugdax/Shutterstock; **p44 (t, l):** Lance Bellers/Shutterstock; **p44 (t, m):** Sergei25/Shutterstock; **p44 (t, r):** DisobeyArt/Shutterstock; **p44 (b, l):** SkyPics Studio/Shutterstock; **p44 (b, r):** BongkarnGraphic/Shutterstock; **p47 (t):** Cagkan Sayin/Shutterstock; **p47 (b):** THEBILLJR/Shutterstock; **p48 (t, l):** Andrey_Popov/Shutterstock; **p48 (t, r):** Bo1982/Shutterstock; **p48 (b, l):** Luoxi/Shutterstock; **p48 (b, r):** Prathankarnpap/Shutterstock; **p50 (l):** Paul Doyle/Alamy Stock Photo; **p50 (m):** Martin Pelanek/Shutterstock; **p50 (r):** Nitul Gogoi PhotoIllustro/Shutterstock; **p51:** Subhrajit123/Shutterstock; **p53:** EkaterinaNovikova/Shutterstock; **p54:** Dragon Images/Shutterstock; **p55 (l):** Jaromir Chalabala/Shutterstock; **p55 (r):** D'Action Images/Shutterstock; **p61:** Tatyana Blinova/Shutterstock; **p62 (t, l):** Nazri Yaakub/Shutterstock; **p62 (t, r):** Mikael Damkier/Shutterstock; **p62 (b, l):** fizkes/Shutterstock; **p62 (b, r):** Bits And Splits/Shutterstock; **p64 (t, l):** Dmitry Rukhlenko/Shutterstock; **p64 (t, r):** PeopleImages.com - Yuri A/Shutterstock; **p64 (b, l):** Andrey_Popov/Shutterstock; **p64 (b, r):** Alena Yudina/Shutterstock; **p65 (t, l):** Bakhtiar Zein/Shutterstock; **p65 (t, r):** ZinetroN/Shutterstock; **p65 (b, l):** Dragana Gordic/Shutterstock; **p65 (b, r):** Slavun/Shutterstock; **p66 (t):** blue-sea.cz/Shutterstock; **p66 (m):** olesea vetrila/Shutterstock; **p66 (b):** Ginnyyj/Shutterstock; **p67 (l):** Piyaset/Shutterstock; **p67 (r):** Bob Daemmrich/Alamy Stock Photo; **p68:** MarLein/Shutterstock; **p69 (t):** Robyn Mackenzie/Shutterstock; **p69 (b):** UfaBizPhoto/Shutterstock; **p70 (t):** LCRP/Shutterstock; **p70 (b):** LongJon/Shutterstock; **p71:** skynesher/getty images; **p72 (t, l):** 4zevar/Shutterstock; **p72 (t, r):** Daisy Daisy/Shutterstock; **p72 (b, l):** airdone/Shutterstock; **p72 (b, r):** GoodStudio/Shutterstock; **p73 (t):** Porcupen/Shutterstock; **p73 (b):** eamesBot/Shutterstock; **p74 (t):** Rus S/Shutterstock; **p74 (b):** natashanast/Shutterstock; **p76:** aappp/Shutterstock; **p77 (t, l):** LightField Studios/Shutterstock; **p77 (t, r):** Charlie Edward/Shutterstock; **p77 (b, l):** Red Stock/Shutterstock; **p77 (b, r):** Kathy images/Shutterstock; **p78 (t):** lechatnoir/Getty Images; **p78 (b):** VectorMine/Shutterstock; **p79 (t):** Antun Hirsman/Shutterstock; **p79 (b):** Natalya Bardushka/Shutterstock; **p80:** GAS-photo/Shutterstock; **p81:** 3rdtimeluckystudio/Shutterstock; **p82 (b):** Vectorium/Shutterstock; **p84 (t):** Aldo Favini/Shutterstock; **p84 (b):** Kalinka Georgieva/Alamy Stock Photo; **p92 (3):** Tupungato/Shutterstock; **p93 (2):** nadtochiy/Shutterstock; **p93 (3):** Elen Marlen/Shutterstock; **p93 (4):** WESTOCK PRODUCTIONS/Shutterstock; **p93 (5):** 1000 Words/Shutterstock; **p93 (6):** Space-kraft/Shutterstock.

Any third party use of this material, outside of this publication, is prohibited. Interested parties should apply to the copyright holders indicated in each case. Although we have made every effort to trace and contact all copyright holders before publication this has not been possible in all cases. If notified, the publisher will rectify any errors or omissions at the earliest opportunity.

The manufacturer's authorised representative in the EU for product safety is Oxford University Press España S.A. of el Parque Empresarial San Fernando de Henares, Avenida de Castilla, 2–28830 Madrid (www.oup.es/en).

Contents

Project framework: IDEAS to Action

The IDEAS to Action Framework is a bit like a map to help you plan your project. There are six steps in the framework. We will cover each of these steps through the Project Book.

1. Investigate: Introduce and learn about a problem

Your goal in this section is to learn the causes and effects of the problem you are trying to solve.

2. Define: Develop solutions

Your goal in this section is to decide how you will approach the problem: what solution do you propose?

3. Explore: Experiment and test solutions

Your goal in this section is to create and test your solution and explore improvements.

4. Act: Apply, engage, and implement your solution

Your goal in this section is to make the project a reality.

5. Share: Reflect, communicate, and consider learnings

Your goal in this section is to take some time to share what you have done and reflect on what you have learned.

6. Go further! Take action for global change

Your goal in this section is to take action in your own community, or in other areas of your life, using the skills you have learned.

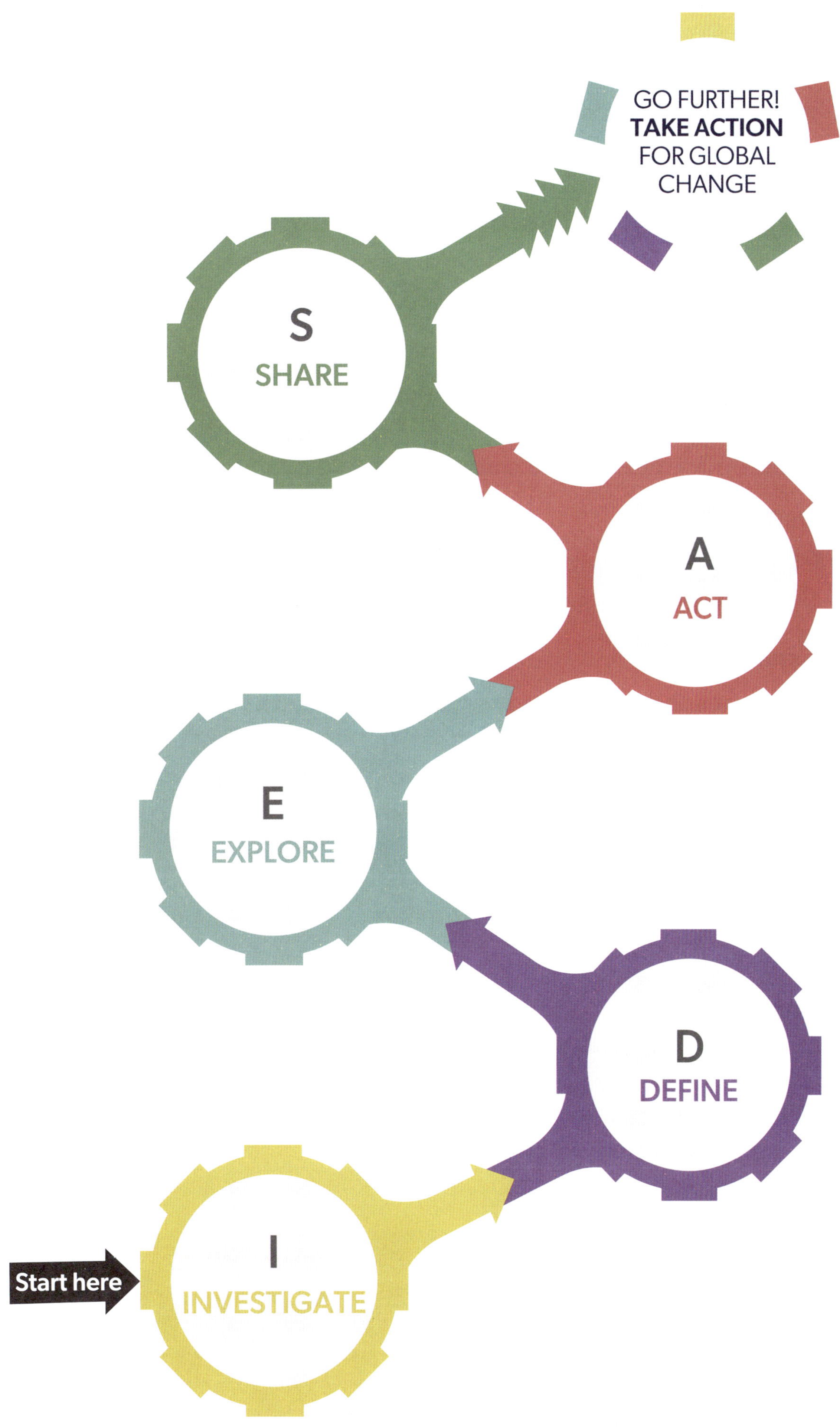

GO FURTHER!
TAKE ACTION
FOR GLOBAL
CHANGE
S
SHARE
A
ACT
E
EXPLORE
D
DEFINE
Start here
I
INVESTIGATE

1 Thriving on Earth

Contents

Dear Student,

Welcome to your first project of Year 9, in which we challenge you to take actions to protect and restore the health of Earth.

In this project, you will learn how to contribute to a sustainable future and how to make change happen. You will look again at the laws and principles from nature that support life on Earth. You will learn how to advocate for why people should understand those laws.

You will consider real-life situations, such as the growing problem of desertification. You will use these examples to learn about living systems, and how healthy living systems live within limits. It's essential to understand and respect those limits if we and Earth are to thrive and have a healthy future.

You will look at other young people who are calling for change. You will then create a campaign designed to protect and restore the health of the ecosystem services on which we depend.

You will also imagine a day in your future life, in which everything you do contributes to your health and the health of Earth. It can be really powerful to imagine your future and use this to set yourself goals.

Have fun exploring and working on your project!

Best wishes,

The Sustainability Team

How does nature behave?

In your Project Notebook, write short answers to these questions:

1. What do we need from nature to survive?

2. Does nature need anything from us?

Food to eat

Clean water to drink

Clean air to breathe

Somewhere safe to live

In this project, you will look at protecting and restoring the health of our Earth. Nature produces life on Earth. Understanding how nature behaves is therefore very important. Complete the activity on page 84–85.

Let's get talking

As a class, discuss the questions to review your ideas about laws and principles.

- What examples of laws can you think of?
- A principle is any idea or belief that guides the way you act and behave. Give an example of a principle that you follow.
- How are laws and principles in nature different to those in society?

Nature's laws and principles

In the introductory activity, we found that:

- people depend on nature to live

- nature does not depend on people.

Even though nature does not depend on us, our actions affect nature. We therefore need to learn how we can contribute to the health of living systems.

Part of being able to protect and restore the health of our Earth is about understanding the laws and principles that nature uses. These laws support life on Earth.

1. **Things are always changing**. Life is dynamic and always evolving.

2. **Life organizes towards life.** Organisms adapt to what is available and make use of whatever they find around them.

3. **Everything must go somewhere because there is no such place as 'away'.**

   - Laws of conservation: Matter and energy are not created or destroyed; they change from one thing to another, or are transferred.

   - Entropy: Materials produced by people eventually fall apart. This can be harmful to our health and the health of our Earth.

4. **Diversity makes our lives possible.** Diversity promotes healthy and resilient ecosystems.

5. **Healthy systems have limits.**

   - The maximum size of a population in an area is determined by the area's resources and what those resources can support. This is known as the carrying capacity.

6. **We are all in this together.** Everything and everyone are interdependent and interconnected.

7. **Solutions are local.** Change happens to fit the unique needs of a particular environment.

When we recognize and work with these laws and principles (rather than against them), we increase our ability to thrive over time.

Check your understanding of these laws and principles. In your Project Notebook, make a table with two columns. Put the seven laws and principles above in the first column. In the second column, add at least one example of your own for each law or principle.

Nature's laws and principles in a local area

Everything on Earth — living and non-living — has to follow the laws and principles that come from nature.

This means that everything in your local area is affected by these laws and principles, including you and everyone else.

Look at the photographs below. They are also examples from a specific, or local, area.

1. Do you think the laws and principles of nature are being followed in each photograph?

2. How do you know?

3. Which laws are, or are not, being followed?

Write down your ideas in your Project Notebook.

In groups, you are going to research examples in your local area. You will link these examples to nature's laws and principles. Each group will research a different law.

Researching local examples

The boxes below will give you some ideas. Write your research in your Project Notebook.

1. Things are always changing.
- Has a change happened in your local area meaning that animals or plants have had to adapt?
- Has there been a change that had a positive or negative effect on other living things?
- If negative, what could be done to improve the situation in the future?

2. Life organizes towards life.
- Was a site in your local area left abandoned and is now home to nature?
- Are there any examples of ecological succession in your local area?
- Can you think of any living thing that has repaired itself to allow it to carry on living?

3. Everything must go somewhere, because there is no such place as 'away'.
- What happens to the rubbish and recyclables in your local area?
- Are there any examples of nature recycling things in your local area?
- Matter and energy are never destroyed; they change form or are transferred elsewhere. Can you relate this idea to anywhere in your local area?

4. Diversity makes our lives possible.
- Are there any diverse wildlife areas locally?
- Where is there less biodiversity in your local area? How could you make those areas more diverse?
- Where is human diversity respected and celebrated in your local area? Why is diversity important?

5. Healthy systems have limits.
- Is there anywhere in your local area where limits have not been respected? Has this had a negative impact on wildlife or plants?
- Can you describe a local food chain or food web? How would it be affected if there were too many or too few of one type of animal in the chain or web?
- Is there a local example where people are respecting nature's limits? Is it having a positive impact?

6. We are all in this together.
- Can you think of any local examples where plants and animals depend on each other to survive?
- Is there anywhere in your local area where people are working with nature rather than against it? What is the effect?

7. Solutions are local.
- Is there anywhere in your community that teaches local knowledge about nature? Examples might be nature walks, information sites, museums, or community leaders.
- Is there anywhere in your community where local actions, which are appropriate to your specific location, are improving the environment?

Now tell the class about your research. As you listen to the other groups, in your Project Notebook write a list of local examples of each of nature's laws and principles.

Why should we all understand nature's laws and principles?

You have learned that when we work with nature's laws and principles (rather than against them), we increase our ability to thrive over time.

What can happen if we don't follow nature's laws and principles?

Thinking about this question can help us to explain why understanding nature's laws and principles is so important.

Work in small groups. In your Project Notebook, write a list of what could happen if we don't follow nature's laws and principles. Make sure you link each idea to a particular law or principle. Use your work from Lesson 1 and 2 to help you.

The following questions and photographs will give you some more clues.

1. What could happen if we always try to do things the same way?

2. What could happen if governments always make the decisions and they don't consider local differences and local knowledge?

3. What could happen if we try to work only by ourselves and don't respect nature, other communities, and other living things?

Pollution from vehicles

Electronic waste in a landfill

Overfishing

You can advocate

You have now thought about some negative consequences of not following nature's laws and principles. It doesn't have to be like that! You can make a difference.

We use the word advocate to describe the action of sharing support for something with the public. If you advocate for something, you are saying why you think that thing is important and why you support it.

Advocating for something can bring about real change.

You are now going to use all your learning from Lesson 1, 2, and 3 to produce your assessed piece of work. Which of the assessment criteria are you aiming for? What do those assessment criteria mean?

Developing	• Say why you think people should understand nature's laws and principles. Explain your ideas as fully as possible and use examples if you can.
Secure	• Persuade people that understanding nature's laws and principles is essential. Explain your ideas as fully as possible. • Support your argument with a local example. Show how that example needs an understanding of nature's laws and principles. You can use examples from around the world as well.
Extending	• Persuade people that understanding nature's laws and principles is essential. Explain your ideas as fully as possible. • Support your argument with a local example. Show how that example needs an understanding of nature's laws and principles. You can use examples from around the world as well. • Deliver your argument to your local government, family or school, and community members. Try to persuade them why understanding nature's laws and principles is essential, and try to bring about change.

You can present your work in any suitable way.

Living within limits

We, and everything around us, live within limits. What would happen if we didn't?

Look at this person below. They need all the things around them to survive. But what would happen if they had too much of one of those things? What would happen if they had too little of one of those things?

A human being is an example of a living system. All living systems have natural limits to keep them balanced. You learned about these in Year 7. Can you remember what they are?

Let's get talking

A drainage basin is an example of a river system. Use the questions to discuss how the system stays in balance.

- What would happen if water was flowing into the system faster than it was moving downstream?
- What would happen if water was flowing out of the system faster than it was flowing in?
- Who or what would be affected by each of these changes?
- How would they be affected?

Consider the consequences on both a local and an international scale. Write your ideas in your Project Notebook.

What does a healthy living system need?

A healthy living system needs just the right balance of things to be able to thrive.

Knowing that there are limits, and what those limits are, can help us to adjust (change) our behaviour. When we adjust our behaviour, we can live well without harming nature.

Two useful ideas to consider when determining the health of a system are:

- **biological capacity** – the ability of an ecosystem to produce useful resources and deal with waste
- **resource replenishment rate** – how quickly and effectively an ecosystem can replace its resources.

If the flow of a resource out of a system is greater than the replenishment rate of that resource, it can affect an area's biological capacity.

Desertification is when land turns into desert because the soil loses its **fertility** over time. Desertification is happening in many dry areas around the world. The photograph and text below give some reasons for desertification.

Growing too many crops (**overcultivation**) means the soil becomes **infertile**.

Overgrazing by animals removes plants which hold the soil together.

Without plants, the soil is not protected and blows away (**soil erosion**).

Climate change means drier conditions.

Larger populations mean people want more wood and water.

Trees are cut down for fuel.

Poor and **unsustainable** farming practices damage the health of the soil.

Let's get talking

Discuss the questions, then write your answers in your Project Notebook.

- Explain how the reasons for desertification can be linked to biological capacity or resource replenishment rate.
- Explain the impacts of desertification on biological capacity.

Healthy systems live within limits

In Lesson 4, you learned that for a healthy living system to thrive, it needs a balance of things. It needs to live within limits.

Are you living within limits? Are you living within Earth's biological capacity and resource replenishment rate? Use the link your teacher gives you to find out.

Then, in your Project Notebook, answer these questions:

1. When was your personal Overshoot Day?

2. What do you think was the main impact on your ecological footprint?

3. What changes will you make to improve your ecological footprint, either yourself, in your family, or in your community?

Let's stop and reflect on what you have learned so far.

Remember that all the living systems on Earth have the opportunity to thrive! If we know the limits, and keep to those limits, the living systems will be very successful.

These are some of the systems that we have looked at so far:

The human body

Rivers

Ecosystems at risk of desertification

Demonstrating your understanding

These are other living systems that you will be familiar with:

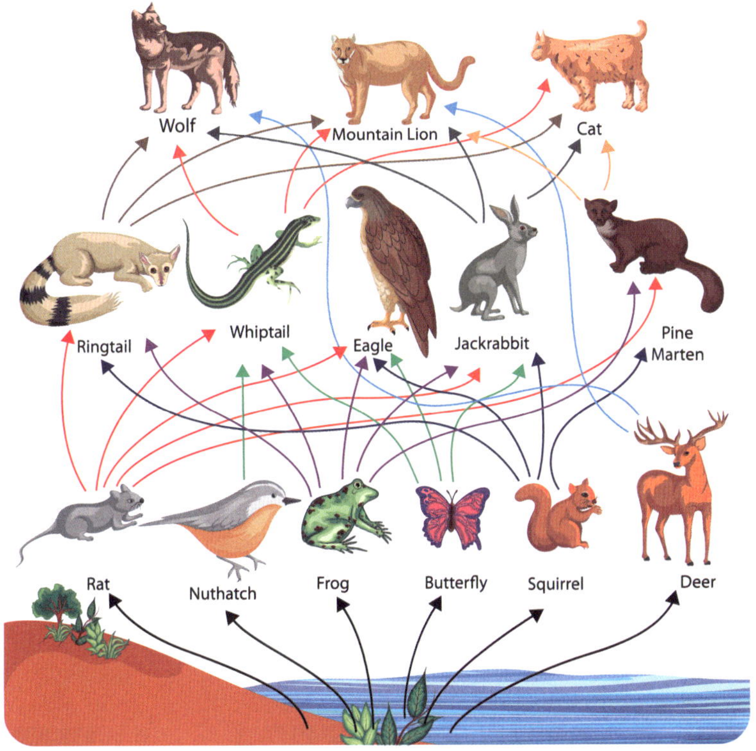

Food webs

Gardens, plants at home, or parks

Farms

There are many other living systems too!

In pairs or small groups, you are going to design a game. Your game will either:

- explain that a healthy living system requires just the right balance of things it needs to be able to thrive (Developing)

or:

- demonstrate your understanding that healthy systems thrive within their biological capacity and resource replenishment rate (Secure and Extending).

If you are aiming for 'Extending', then you will also need to model a healthy living system that is 'tapping the power of limits'. Your teacher will give you guidance on how to do this.

First, design your game by drawing pictures of what it will look like or by writing down instructions. Then, if there is time, swap your design with another group and discuss each other's ideas.

The ecosystem services we depend on

You studied ecosystem services in Year 8. Can you remember what ecosystem services are?

In your Project Notebook, make a list of ten ways in which you have used ecosystem services in the past week. Make sure you link each activity to a particular ecosystem service.

Share your list with a partner. How similar are your lists? Can you add to your list after hearing your partner's ideas?

Some of the ecosystem services that we depend on are not always healthy. You learned in Year 8 that ecosystem services are affected by the behaviour of humans. Use the photographs below and the activity on page 86–87 to explain how the health of some ecosystem services are threatened by humans. Add in further ideas of your own, if you can. Think back to your work in previous lessons to help you.

Although pesticides help to protect crops, they can have damaging effects on other parts of the environment.

Some leisure activities, such as offroad driving and quad biking, can have big impacts on the natural environment.

We use electricity for many things but creating electricity often involves burning fossil fuels.

Protecting and restoring the health of ecosystem services

Reflect on how you feel after the previous activity. Think about how humans have worked together to restore the health of one ecosystem service.

You are now going to consider other strategies that could be used to protect and restore the health of ecosystem services.

- Choose one ecosystem service to focus on to begin with.
- Any solutions do not have to be international! Local solutions are also very effective strategies.

Work in pairs to think of at least one strategy that could be used to protect and restore the health of an ecosystem service. Write your ideas in your Project Notebook.

Use the flow diagram on this lesson's activity page to test your idea and check that it could work. Using SMART targets for your solution is a good way to keep your solution achievable.

Your solution should be:

specific: make sure you give enough details and information

measurable: your progress and success can be measured

achievable: your solution can be achieved or completed

realistic: the solution is possible in this situation

timely: the solution can be achieved by a certain time.

What is a campaign?

A campaign is a planned series of actions that are designed to achieve a particular goal.

You are going to create a campaign to protect and restore the health of ecosystem services.

Other young people have run successful campaigns before.

Autumn Peltier is an Anishinaabe Indigenous rights and water conservation advocate from the Wiikwemkoong First Nation in Canada. She began campaigning for the universal right to clean drinking water when she was very young. She has raised awareness towards water rights through petitions, social media, and by speaking at important forums, both nationally and internationally.

Felix Finkbeiner, from Germany, started the organization Plant-for-the-Planet at age 9. He has spoken at the United Nations General Assembly and says that we should plant 1 trillion trees by 2050.

Ridhima Pandey is a young climate activist from India. She has been involved in action against climate change since she was 9 years old. This includes calling for a complete ban on plastic.

In your Project Notebook, make a list of the different ways in which these young people have run their campaigns.

Discuss your list with a partner. What other ways can you think of to run a campaign? Add these ideas to your list.

Discuss the questions your teacher gives you and write your answers in your Project Notebook.

Planning your campaign

You are going to plan a campaign to protect and restore the health of ecosystem services.

1. Choose one or two ecosystem services. A focused campaign will work better than one that tries to cover everything.

2. Decide whether you are going to focus on a local ecosystem service or a larger one. Consider what might work best for a successful campaign. Which ecosystem service will your campaign be most effective at helping? For example:

Will your campaign encourage people to pick up litter and not to create litter?

Will your campaign encourage people to plant trees?

Will your campaign aim to reduce the use of plastic?

Choose ecosystem services and issues that are important to you.

You can work individually, in pairs, or in small groups.

First, plan your ideas using the activity on page 88–89.

You will then use your answers to prepare the resources for your campaign in the next lesson.

What makes an effective campaign?

Compare the two emails below. Which one might be more effective for a campaign? Why?

> ✉ New message — ↗ ×
>
> Please will you increase the number of bus services in our area? I think that will help to reduce climate change. Reducing climate change is really important.

> ✉ New message — ↗ ×
>
> According to *The Sustainable Development Goals Report 2022*, 'the global annual average temperature is predicted to rise beyond 1.5 °C above pre-industrial levels in at least one of the next five years'. Global climate change is having serious impacts on coral reefs and is causing increased levels of flooding in some areas and droughts in others.
>
> We have the ability to do something about this. I suggest that we immediately increase the number of bus services in our area so that they run every 30 minutes. At present, there is one bus that runs every two hours into the nearest town. This is not enough. As a result, people are using their cars to make short journeys and releasing more greenhouse gases into the atmosphere. By increasing the frequency of bus services, people are more likely to take the bus than use their cars.

You are going to create your campaign. Use your ideas from the work you have done in the past two lessons. Remember:

1. Keep the message simple.

2. Aim to persuade other people to make a positive change.

3. Link your campaign clearly to protecting and restoring the health of at least one ecosystem service.

It is important at all stages that you consider risks. Do not do anything unsafe or illegal. Check with your teacher if you are not sure. Think back to your discussions in Lesson 7. What other risks should you think about?

Creating your campaign

Create your campaign by writing your emails, creating your videos, drawing your posters, or producing anything else that you need for your campaign.

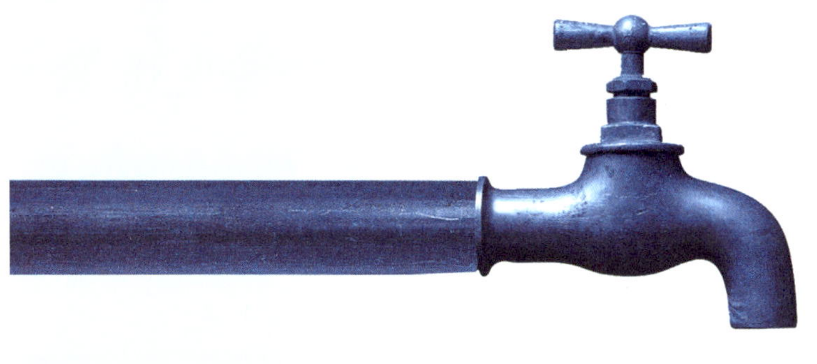

When you have finished creating the materials for your campaign, show them to the class and explain what you have done.

Finally, reflect on your work. In your Project Notebook, write down one thing about your campaign that you are proud of.

Imagining your future life

Imagine your life in 20 years' time.

Think about the following questions:

What will you eat and drink?

What will your job be?

How will you travel around?

What will you do in your leisure time?

What will your home be like? Where will it be?

Use the 'First ideas' boxes on your activity on page 90–91 to write down your answers to these questions. (Leave the 'Second ideas' boxes blank for now.)

How can we contribute to our health and the health of Earth?

Imagine a future where everything we do contributes to our health and the health of Earth.

Look at the 'First ideas' you wrote on your activity. How many of those ideas are good for your health and the health of Earth? How many are not?

In groups, you are going to think of solutions. These solutions will mean that people are improving their own health and the health of Earth.

The questions below will give you some clues to think about. Your teacher will tell you which theme your group will start with. Your teacher will rotate the groups so that you get a chance to add your solutions to the list for each theme.

Home
- What sustainable building materials will your home be made from? How will you use efficient and renewable energy?
- How will you make sure that your home contributes to the health of the ecosystem services on which we depend?

Job
- How will you make sure that your job contributes to your health and wellbeing?
- Will you choose a job which directly helps to improve people's health and the health of Earth?
- If not, how can you make sure that your job still contributes to your health and the health of Earth?

Transport
- What are the forms of transport that contribute to the health of Earth?
- Are any of these forms of transport better for your health too?
- How will you make sure that you are still able to get where you need to go?

Leisure time
- What activities can you do that will benefit your own health?
- What activities can you do that will benefit the health of Earth?
- For all other activities, how can you make sure that they contribute to your health and the health of Earth upon which we depend?

Food and drink
- Where will you buy your food and drink?
- How will you make sure that your food and drink contributes to reversing global warming?
- How will you make sure that your food and drink contributes to the health of the ecosystem services?

We can improve our ideas when we ask questions about why we think what we do, and suggest alternatives.

Now use the 'Second ideas' box on your activity to say how your future life can contribute more to our health and the health of Earth.

Your vision for your future life

Having a clear vision for the future helps you to achieve your goals and get to where you want to be.

How might the world be different if all young people had a vision to live a life that benefits their health and the health of Earth?

Imagine your future self and think carefully. The more you keep that sustainable future in your mind, the more it will seem possible and you will take steps to achieve it.

Keeping that vision in mind will help you to achieve a sustainable future.

Look at the photographs below. Explain how each one shows people contributing to their health and/or the health of Earth.

An **urban** garden in Bangkok, Thailand

Solar power being **generated** in rural Uganda

Volunteers building **affordable** housing in
Soweto, South Africa

Describing your future life

In your Project Notebook, write a story describing a day in your future life. You could write it as:

- a diary entry

- a story

- a letter or an email to a friend.

Use your ideas from Lesson 9 and this lesson. Make sure your description shows how you contribute to your health and the health of Earth.

If you are aiming for 'Extending' on the assessment criteria, then think also about when you will publish your story in a local school or community paper. You can share what you have done in the next lesson.

Swap your finished story with a partner. Read your partner's story and give feedback on the following:

- One thing in their story that you think will contribute most to their health or the health of Earth.

- Why that thing will be a particularly strong contribution.

- One thing that they could improve to contribute even more to their health or the health of Earth.

- Explain why that improvement will contribute even more.

Then reflect on the feedback you received.

Reflecting on your learning

Think about what you have learned or achieved during this project.

Advocate for why people should understand the laws and principles from nature that support life on Earth.	
You have: • identified the laws and principles from nature that support life on Earth • learned why it is important to understand those laws and principles • learned how to advocate for those laws and principles, using a local example.	You may also have: • advocated for that understanding to your local government, family or school, and community members.*
Understand that healthy systems live within the biological capacity and resource replenishment rates.	
You have: • learned some examples of living systems • learned how healthy living systems live within limits (biological capacity and resource replenishment rate) • designed a game to show your understanding of how healthy living systems live within limits.	You may also have: • shown how a healthy living system is 'tapping the power of limits'.
Create a campaign to protect and restore the health of the ecosystem services that we depend on.	
You have: • considered how ecosystem services are at risk • learned strategies that could be used to protect and restore the health of ecosystem services • created a campaign to protect and restore the health of ecosystem services.	You may also have: • run the campaign to protect and restore the health of ecosystem services in your local community.
Describe a day in your future life in which everything you do contributes to your health and the health of our Earth.	
You have: • imagined your future life • worked together to create solutions to make sure your future life will be contributing to your health and the health of Earth • described a day in your future life in which everything you do contributes to your health and the health of Earth.	You may also have: • published your story in a local school or community paper.

* The points in the second column are things you may have done in your own time at home.

Reflect on your work with a partner. Use the questions your teacher gives you to help you.

Sharing the lessons

You are now going to share what you have learned during this project.

If you have **not** done any of the points in the second column in the table opposite, create a short drama sketch.

- This sketch should teach students in another class or year group one of the most important lessons that you have learned.
- Make sure the message or lesson that you want to pass on is clear.
- If there are many different ideas in your group, choose one idea to focus on.

If you **have** done any of the points in the second column in the table:
- Prepare a short presentation to share what you did with the class.
- Use the questions belows to see what your presentation should include.

   1. What exactly did you do?
   2. Did you have any response to your actions?
   3. How successful did you feel your actions were?
   4. What could you do differently next time to improve the outcome even further?

As you are working together on your drama or presentation, take time on your own at least once to think about the following questions:

1. Are we working well together?
2. Are my teammates willing to listen to me and consider my suggestions?
3. Am I able to consider new ideas raised by my teammates, even if they contradict my own? Is this difficult for me?
4. What role am I playing in the group? Am I happy with this role?
5. Is there anything that needs to change about our group dynamic?

You will present your drama sketches or presentations to other students. They will give you feedback based on the following questions. Read these before you start planning your work.

   1. How clear was the information or message being presented?
   2. Did everyone contribute equally to the drama sketch or presentation?
   3. Did everybody speak clearly and confidently?
   4. Did everybody know what their role was in the drama sketch or presentation?

Watch the other groups' sketches or presentations. While you watch, make notes on the above questions. You can also make notes on anything else that you think the groups have done well.

From your classroom to the wider world

In this project, you have learned about protecting and restoring the health of Earth.

1. You have advocated for why people should understand nature's laws and principles.

2. You have understood that healthy systems live within the biological capacity and resource replenishment rates.

3. You have created a campaign to protect and restore the health of the ecosystem services on which we depend.

4. You have described a day in your future life in which everything you do contributes to your health and the health of Earth.

Take some time to think through what you have learned in this project. Write down your answers to the following questions in your Project Notebook:

1. What are you most proud of in this project?

2. What skill(s) do you think you developed through this project?

3. What would you like to continue to learn to develop your knowledge further? (This could be a skill or a topic.)

Setting goals

Although your project is finished, your ability to learn about protecting and restoring the health of Earth continues!

In your Project Notebook, write down some short-, medium-, and long-term goals for yourself, to make sure you keep learning, or that you take action to have a positive impact. Below are some examples to get you thinking.

Short-term goal:

Example: In the next two weeks, I will show my drama or presentation from Lesson 11 to a different group of students, my family, or somebody else in my community. I will help to spread the important lessons that I have learned.

____

____

Medium-term goal:

Example: Over the next six months, I will continue to run my campaign to protect and restore the health of ecosystem services. I will track how effective the campaign is and make changes to connect with as many people as possible.

____

____

Long-term goal:

Example: By the time I am in my 30s, I want to be living the life I described in my story, where everything I do contributes to my health and the health of Earth.

____

____

Think about what you need to do to carry out these goals, and work hard to do it! And finally, try to do something positive for Earth every day!

2 Tracking the health of a local commons

Contents

Dear Student,

Welcome to your second project of Year 9, in which we challenge you to track the health of a local commons.

In this project, you will create and implement a plan which will make a real difference in your community! To do that, you will work through each learning outcome.

First, you will consider which indicators can measure the health of a local commons. You will discuss how to collect the data we need to measure the health of our commons over time. You will then collect that baseline data and make it visible to your community.

Second, you will consider different ways to protect or improve the health of our community. Which methods are the best? Why? You will evaluate the methods and try to choose the best ones in your plan.

Third, you will work together to write a plan. This plan will give you the opportunity to care for a local commons that we depend on and are responsible for. It will give you the opportunity to make a positive change in your community.

Finally, you will develop and implement that plan. You will make the changes needed. You will measure the progress of your plan against the baseline data you collected. You will also make sure that you involve and educate the community so that the benefits of your plan reach as far as possible.

Have fun exploring and working on your project!

Best wishes,

The Sustainability Team

Tracking the health of your local commons

Where are your local commons?

Can you name any examples of these commons in your local area?

Work in small groups to complete question 1 on your activity on page 92–93.

It is important to track the health of our local commons. If we track their health, we can:

- do more of the behaviour that is helping to protect the commons and keep it healthy, or
- change our behaviour if the health of the commons is getting worse.

To track a commons' health, we need to use data to measure its health. Indicators are data that can be used to track the commons' health.

For example, to track the health of the air in our local area, an indicator would be the amount of air pollutants in the atmosphere.

Commons: air

Indicator: the amount of air pollutants

Some of this data may already have been collected by others and can be researched. For example, you can use data collected by others to research the air quality in your area.

In your groups, complete question 2 on your activity.

Remember, indicators might be data that somebody has already collected, or data that hasn't been collected yet but should be.

Discuss your answers as a class.

Choosing the commons you want to protect

During this project, you are going to write and implement a plan to care for a local commons. Part of being able to care for this commons is to track its health over time. This process involves:

- collecting a set of data as baseline data.
- continuing to collect more sets of data over time to see what changes are happening.

First, you need to choose which local commons you want to protect.

What will you choose?

Public transport?

The local park?

Local culture, traditions, and knowledge?

Insects and plants in your area?

Or another local commons?

In small groups:

1. Choose the local commons that you want to protect.

2. Decide on up to three indicators that you could use to track that commons' health.

3. Use the example your teacher gives you to think about how you could collect data for your indicators. You will start to collect your data in Lesson 2.

Write down your ideas to all three points in your Project Notebook.

Data collection methods

In Lesson 1, you looked at indicators to measure and track the health of a local commons. You thought of some ways in which data can be collected. You could research data that somebody else has collected (secondary data). Or you could collect the data yourself (primary data).

Here are some primary data collection methods:

Counts: This is to find out the number of something, for example the number of pedestrians (people walking) using a traffic-free area, or the number of butterflies in a green space. You could use a tally chart to record the number that you see in a certain amount of time.

Questionnaires: These can be used to ask people's opinions about things. Questions can be closed (Have you travelled by bus today? Yes/No) or open (Why have you travelled by bus today?).

Interviews: Interviews also help to find out people's opinions. The questions are usually open, to allow for longer discussions and answers.

Land use survey: This is when you walk down a street and note down what each of the different buildings are used for. You could mark your answers on a map using a key, or do a tally.

Rating system: Examples might include an Environmental Quality Survey or a Quality/Decay Index.

- For an Environmental Quality Survey, you could visit different areas and give them a rating between −3 and +3 based on factors such as litter, open spaces, the condition of buildings, and so on.
- For a Quality/Decay Index, you could look at a specific type of building in different areas and give it a score between 1 and 10, depending on how well people are looking after it and how attractive it is.

Photographs: Photographs provide evidence. You can annotate them to draw attention to what you have noticed.

Field sketch: Field sketches work in a similar way to photographs, except they are drawn and annotated at the site.

What other methods can you think of? Which method(s) will you use to collect your data?

Now, in your groups, answer questions 1, 2, and 3 on the activity on page 94.

Your teacher will share information with you about sampling strategies.

Now answer questions 4 and 5 on your activity.

Staying safe

It's important to think about how to stay safe before collecting data.

In your group, complete **Part 1 — Staying safe** of the activity on page 95. The photographs below will give you some suggestions.

Share your answers as a class. Add any other ideas to your list that you hadn't thought of.

How could you minimize these risks?

On your activity, write down how you will minimize all the risks that you thought of.

You are now going to practise collecting data.

- You are going to look out of your classroom window, or go outside in your school environment, and count how many birds, insects, or other wildlife that you see.
- Do the count for five minutes.
- Record your scores in a tally on **Part 2 — Wildlife count** of your activity.

Before the next lesson, collect the data you need to measure the health of your chosen local commons. Collect primary data only if it is appropriate for you to do so.

Presenting data

Making data visible helps us, and others, to track the health of our commons over time.

Data should be presented in a suitable way to make the data easier to understand.

Look at the following data presentation techniques which you studied in Year 8.

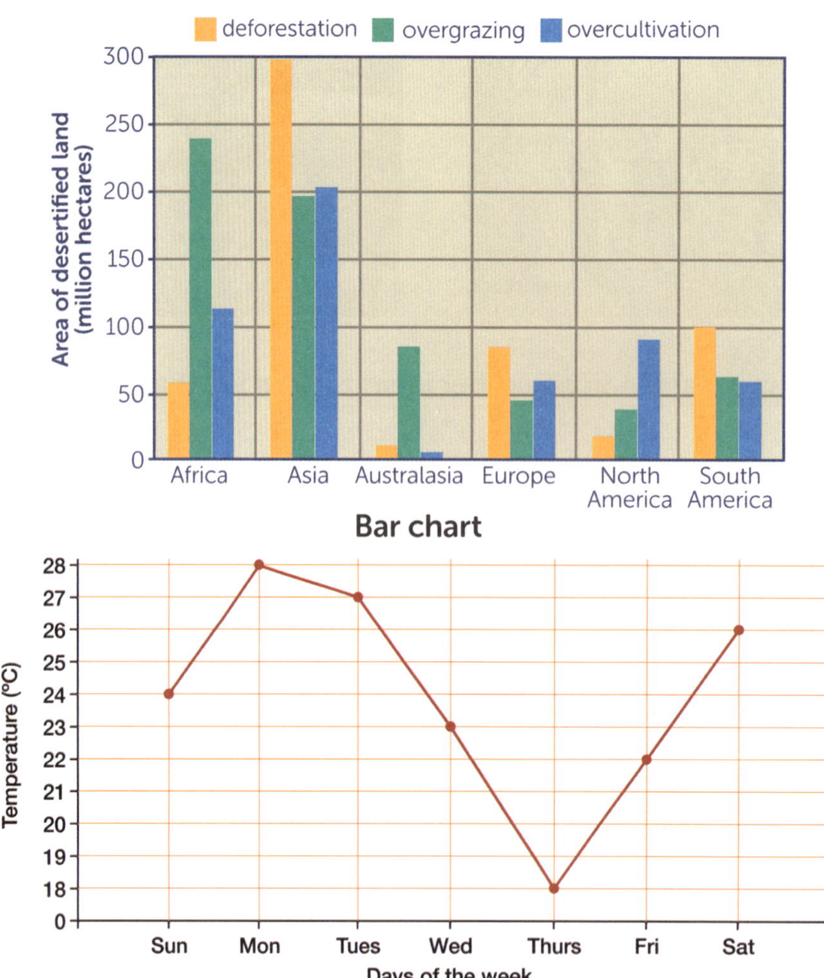

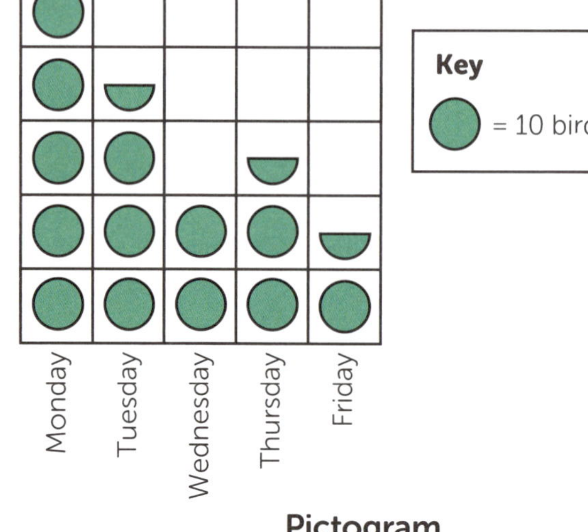

Do you know what each of these data presentation techniques is used for? Do you know of any other suitable data presentation techniques? What are they used for? Share these with the class.

Since Lesson 2, you have collected data to track the health of a local commons over time. This will form your baseline data. You will then see if any changes happen in the data during this project and into the future. You may need to do further data presentation techniques later in the project.

1. In pairs, discuss what the best technique would be to present the baseline data that you have collected.

2. Now draw the graph or other data presentation method to present your data.

Let's get talking

Making data visible means ensuring that other people will see it. 'Data' could be the actual data collected, or the completed graph or other data presentation technique.

- What could you do with your data to make sure people see it?
- What are the positives and negatives of each method?

Discuss your ideas with a partner first and then share with the class.

Why is it important to make data visible? For example, how many people will see the data if you make it visible, compared with if you didn't? What might those people do if they see the data you have collected?

Write down two or three sentences in your Project Notebook to explain why it is so important to make data visible.

If you are aiming for 'Secure' or 'Extending', make the data that you have collected visible. Add some writing with your data to help people understand the data and take action where appropriate. For example:

- What does your data show?
- Why is that important?
- What could people do to take positive actions?

Evaluating ways to improve health

On a piece of paper, write down a list of things you could do to protect or improve your own physical and mental health as you get older. The images below will give you some ideas. Leave some room on the paper in between each item on the list.

Does diet make a difference?

What about staying fit?

Or how you spend your time?

What about socializing with other people?

What else can you think of?

When you have finished your list, cut out each separate item on your list.

With a partner, put the list in order with the most effective method at the top, and the least effective method at the bottom.

How did you decide? What makes a measure more or less effective?

The same principles apply when we protect or improve the health of our community.

Think about what you have learned in Lesson 1–3, and in previous years.

How can we protect or improve the health of our community?

Improving the health of your community

In your Project Notebook, write a list of other ways we can protect or improve the health of our community. The photographs below will give you some ideas. Remember that the health of our community includes all three of the following factors:

- social
- economic
- environmental.

Discuss your ideas as a class.

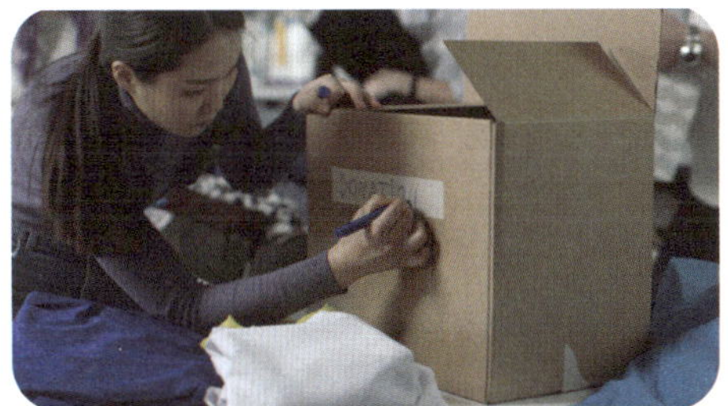

Are there any organizations in your community that need support? Would volunteer work help?

Are there enough sustainable jobs in your area?

What would help to protect and improve the environment in your community?

How would you evaluate those methods? Think back to how you evaluated methods to protect or improve your own health. What questions did you ask yourself? Can any of those questions apply to the health of your community?

As a class, write a list of criteria that you can use to evaluate the ways of protecting and improving the health of the community.

Let's get talking

Use these questions to help you.

- Will the method produce the results you want?
- How likely is it that people will use this method?
- Is the method good value for money?
- How many people would need to be engaged for this method to work?
- How much time will the method take?
- Will the method need investment? From whom?
- Does the method help the entire community or just certain parts?
- What other ideas can you think of?

Now complete the activity on page 96.

How have others tended to a local commons?

Over the next three lessons, you are going to write a plan to tend to the local commons that you care about.

Listen to the story your teacher tells you. Then answer the questions about the story in your Project Notebook.

Over the past four lessons, you have:

- collected data to track the health of a local commons
- evaluated ways to protect or enhance the health of your community.

Try to use all these ideas over the remaining lessons in this project.
When you write – and then implement – your plan, you have the power to make real positive change!

In your groups, work through the following steps:

Step 1: In your Project Notebook, write the heading **Developing our plan – Part 1**. Underneath, write the commons that your group has chosen.

Step 2: Decide: What is your end goal for the local commons you are tending to? What do you want to achieve?

In the story you heard, the girls wanted to:

- put solar panels on all public buildings in their area
- protect the forest near one their homes.

These were their end goals. It is important to think about what you want to achieve before you start, so that you can then work out the steps to get there.

Under **Developing our plan** in your Project Notebook, add the end goal that you want to achieve.

Making a list of essential questions

Before campaigning for solar panels on all public buildings, the girls in the story would have needed to ask lots of questions.

Look at the mind map below to see what kinds of questions the girls might have asked.

What questions do you need to think of for your local commons?

Step 3: Think of questions that need to be asked.

1. In your groups, think of questions you need to ask before you can tend to your local commons. Write your ideas on your **Developing our plan** document.

2. Once you have finished your list, discuss the questions your teacher gives you.

3. Check your list of questions again. Do you need to change any of them? Or do you need to add any more questions?

You will need the work from this lesson for Lesson 6 and 7.

What are the answers to your questions?

In Lesson 5, you:

- reminded yourselves which local commons you want to tend to
- decided on an end goal for that local commons
- wrote some questions that need to be answered before you can tend to the commons.

You need to know the answers to your questions to write a clear plan that shows you have thought carefully about the topic.

For example, who sets the rules for your commons?

Local government?

Private businesses?

Parents/children?

Are the kind of agreements that are needed to tend the commons formal or informal?

In your groups, research the answers to the questions you wrote in Lesson 5.

Write the answers to your questions in your Project Notebook.

Other things to consider

Now that you have answered your questions, work as a group to note down any other details you need to include or things you need to think about for your plan.

1. Look back at your end goal for your local commons. What do you want to achieve?

2. What are the smaller tasks that you need to do to achieve that end goal?

For example, the flow diagram below shows the different steps the girls in the story needed to take to save the forest near to their home.

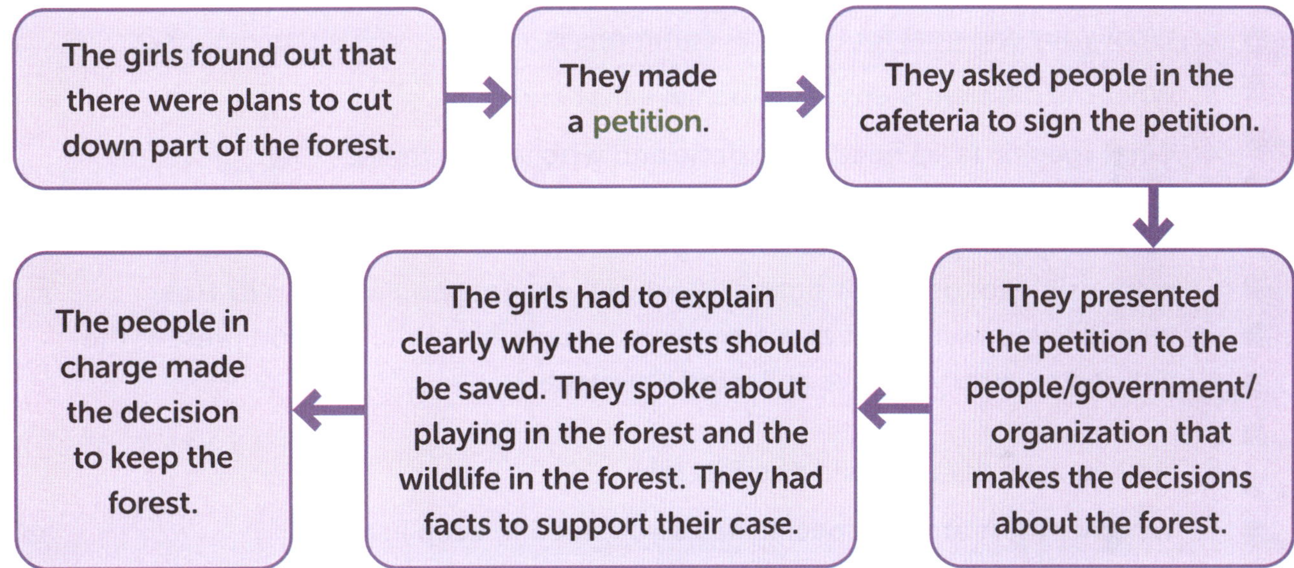

Let's get talking

What steps will you take to achieve your end goal? These steps will be written into your plan in the next lesson.

Think about questions such as:

- What background research might you still need to do?
- What are the different steps to take?
- How long will the actions take that you need to do?
- Does anyone else need to be involved? If so, who?
- How will you approach people that are needed?

Work in your groups to discuss what steps you might want to include in your plan, and what you need to think about. Write down your ideas in your Project Notebook.

You will be writing the plan in Lesson 7.

Writing your plan

In this lesson, you are going to write your plan.

Use all your knowledge from Lesson 1–6. Make sure your plan is clear enough that somebody who is not in your group could still follow it.

You can decide how you present your plan. You need to produce one plan for your whole group. Think how you are going to divide the tasks up so that everybody is involved.

Remember to include the following ideas in your plan:

1. Which local commons you are going to tend to.

2. What your end goal for the local commons is.

3. What the different steps are to achieve that end goal.

4. What specific tasks need to be done and who will do them.

    For example, if you need to write a petition, who will write it? Who will be responsible for getting it signed? How will you get people to sign it? How long will you wait to get as many names as possible? Who will you present the petition to, after you have collected the names?

5. How long each task could possibly take.

6. Whether there are any specific dates you need to keep in mind.

    For example, is there a town meeting coming up where you need to speak to people in charge? What date is that? How are you going to make sure that you have everything ready before that point?

7. The dates by which you need to have completed each task.

8. Extending: Why the steps you are going to follow are the most appropriate ways to protect or improve the health of the commons you have chosen.

Now write your plan in your Project Notebook. Include the local commons you have chosen, your end goal, and a table to show the steps that are needed to achieve the goal.

Task	Who will do the task	Date to achieve the task

Peer-marking your plans

Sometimes, when we look at our own work, it isn't always easy to see what we could do to make it better.

When somebody else looks at our work, they might be able to make suggestions that we had not thought of.

Swap your plan with another group.

Read through their plan and think about the following questions:

1. Is their plan easy to follow?

2. Is it clear who is doing which tasks and when they must be done by?

3. Have they missed out any steps which you think are important?

4. Are all the steps helping them achieve their end goal?

5. Does their end goal help to tend to the local commons?

Write down any feedback in your Project Notebook.

Share your feedback with the original group. Tell them what is good about the plan as well as what could be improved. Remember to give feedback with kindness and tact. Imagine you are them and think about how it will feel to hear what you say. Be truthful but be helpful.

Revisit your plan. Are there any changes you need to make based on the feedback you have received?

Take the opportunity to make those changes.

Implementing your plan

In this lesson you are going to implement your plan. This means you are going to do the actions that you said you would.

You might need to do one of the following:

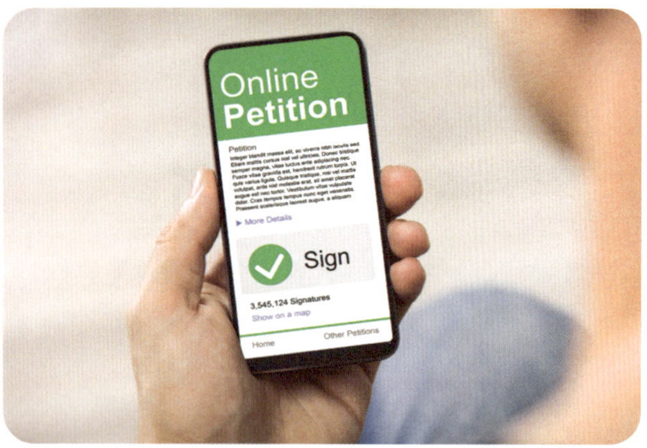

Create a petition, either online or on paper

Write to or email people

Make posters

Prepare a presentation

Or a range of other things.

Spend this lesson doing the things you need to do to action your plan.

Remember to give clear tasks so that everyone in your group is involved.

Checking on your progress

In the middle of the lesson, pause and think about how your group is progressing.

Look at the questions below and see how well you are getting on.

- Are you all working well as a team and doing the same amount of work?

- Can you do anything as a team to work better?

- Is it likely that you will meet the time targets that you put in your plan?

- Do you need to set tasks for yourselves to do at home?

- Are there any problems that you hadn't planned for?

- How can you find solutions to these problems?

- Do you need to ask for help from anybody else?

- Do you need to make any changes to your plan because of anything new from this lesson?

If things are not working out as planned, do not be afraid to admit mistakes. Think about where it has gone wrong and why, and then take action to solve the issues. It is easier to make changes now, before you have finished your project.

How we can measure progress

In Lesson 8, you started to implement your plan. It may be a while before you see the results of your actions. Think back to the baseline data that you collected in Lesson 2.

- How can you now measure the progress of your plan?
- How will you know if your plan is making the difference that you want it to?

Remember what you thought about when you considered how to track the health of your commons over time.

Think back to the story from page 42 again. How do you think the girls could have measured their progress?

The way that you measure the progress of your plans will be focused on what your plans contain. Look at the ideas below. Could any of those be adapted to measure the progress of your plan?

Count how many people have signed a petition.

Continue with wildlife counts to see if numbers have improved. How often would you need to do these counts? Would you need anyone else to help?

Get feedback from the local government office or community-based organization. How often would you want to check? How long might it be until results are achieved?

What other ideas can you think of?

Work in your groups to decide how you are going to measure the progress of your plan. Include ideas about how you will know if your plan has made the difference that you want it to. Link this back to your baseline data and how you will know if progress is being made.

Write your ideas in your Project Notebook.

Involving and educating the community – Part 1

Implementing your plans may create great positive change.

Can you now spread your message even further? Even after you have finished your project, can you tell others what you have done, what you have found out, and why this is important?

By involving and educating the community, you could:

* encourage the community to make further changes
* make it more likely that the community will support the changes that you have made or want to make.

How could you involve and educate the community about your plan?

* Is there a future community event or meeting that you could speak at? If not, could you organize one?
* Is there a local website, newspaper, or TV channel that you could share your story with?
* Could you talk to people, or hand out leaflets, in your community?
* Could you talk to your family and ask each member of your family to then pass on the message to somebody else?

In your groups, think about ways in which you can involve and educate the community about your plan. Remember, this may involve completing more updated data presentation techniques, and making those visible like you did before.

To achieve 'Secure' and 'Extending', you will need not just to think about how to measure progress, and involve and educate the community. You will need to do it!

There will be time to prepare resources to involve and educate the community in Lesson 11. You will need to measure progress in your own time.

Decide as a group how you are going to measure progress before the next lesson.

What we did and why we did it

In this lesson, you will write a report about how you implemented your plans. You will include the following:

1. Method
2. Results
3. Conclusion.

We will discuss each of these sections before you write them.

In your Project Notebook, write the aim of your project. What was your end goal? What were you hoping to achieve?

1. Method

In this section, you will write about:

- what you did
- why you did it
- how you did it.

It needs to be in enough detail that somebody else could repeat the actions that you took. Discuss the example methods your teacher gives you.

Look at the mind map below. It will give you some example questions that you could answer as part of your method.

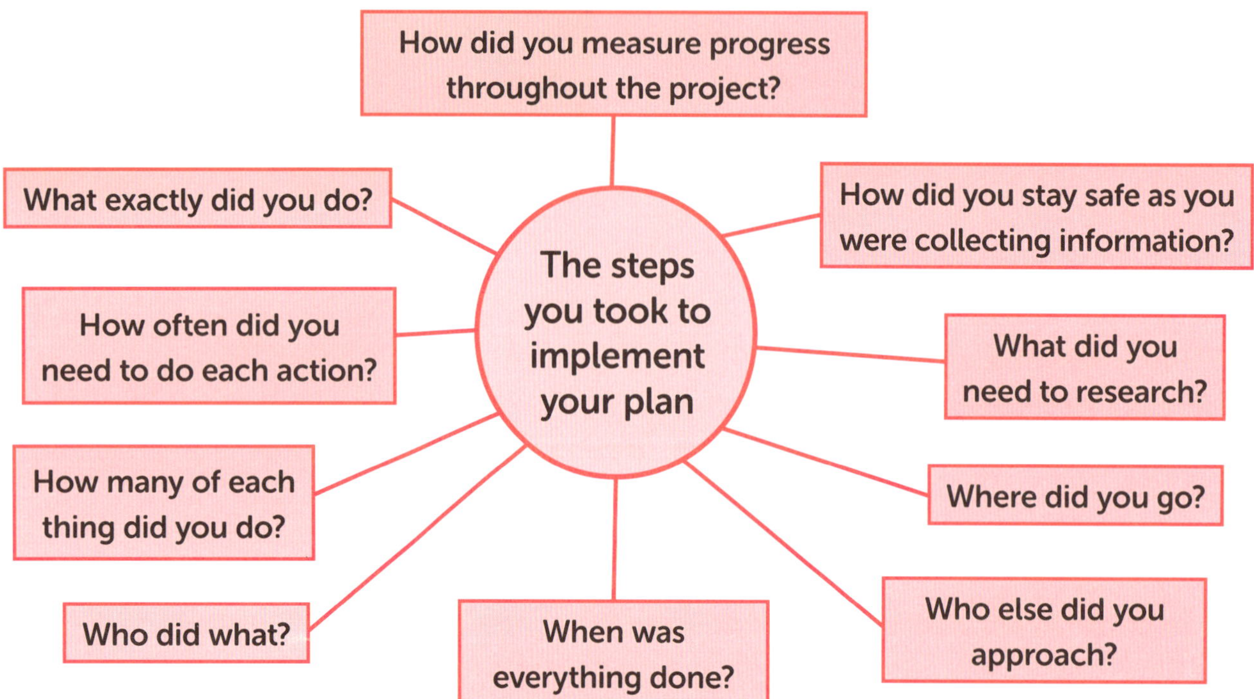

These are just some example questions. Choose the ones that are appropriate to your project. Write the information that is relevant to you.

Now, write your method in your Project Notebook. You can use the activity on page 97 as a guide.

The changes we have seen

2. Results

In this section, you will write about:

- what you found out
- what changes you have seen

This section also needs to be detailed. Include any data you have collected as well.

For example:

- What progress has been made?
- Are things better, the same, or worse than they were before? For example, if you were campaigning for solar panels, how many solar panels are there now compared to when you started your project?
- How do you know?
- Have you changed anyone's opinions? How do you know?

3. Conclusions

This section is a summary of what you have achieved.

For example:

- Have you managed to achieve your end goal?
- How do you know?
- If you haven't, how close are you?
- What else needs to be achieved?
- Are you making progress towards achieving your end goal?

Some projects will take longer than others, depending on what your end goal is. If you haven't achieved your end goal yet, that's okay. Instead, it is important to reflect on:

- what you have achieved so far
- what is left to achieve
- how you are going to make sure that you do achieve your end goal.

Write your results and conclusion in your Project Notebook, after your method. You can use the activity on page 98 to guide you.

Involving and educating the community – Part 2

In Lesson 9, you discussed ways in which your group could involve and educate the community about your project.

Now is your opportunity to do it!

What are you going to do?

For example, you could:

- prepare the speech or presentation that needs to be delivered
- write the article to go on the website or in the local newspaper
- design the leaflets or posters that you need to share information with people.

Or prepare any other resources that you need to send out your message.

Staying safe in the community

In Lesson 2, we discussed the importance of staying safe and considering the risks whenever you go out in the community.

Revisiting this information regularly will help you to remember it every time you do work in the community.

Look at the following ways of staying safe.

- Don't meet a stranger on your own. Stay in groups of three or more.
- Always tell a responsible adult:
    o who you are planning to meet
    o where you have arranged to meet them
    o how long you plan to be.
- Check that you have permission to post anything on a noticeboard or website, or to speak at an event.
- Always be polite and show respect.
- Be prepared for any weather.

What other strategies can you think of to minimize risk?

If you are aiming for 'Secure' or 'Extending', you now need to involve and educate the community using whatever resources you have prepared. You may need to do some of this in your own time.

Celebrating your achievements!

In this project you have:

1. collected and made visible data to track the health of a local commons over time
2. evaluated some ways in which we can protect or improve the health of our community
3. written a plan to care for a local commons that we depend on and are responsible for
4. developed and implemented your plan. Measured the progress of that project over time. Involved and educated the community about your project.

All of you will have done slightly different things. Now is the time to celebrate your achievements and report back about anything you have done outside of lesson times. You will also think about how you can continue to take your learning further.

Developing

1. What are you most proud of in this project and why?
2. What new skills did you learn in this project?
3. Did anything not work in this project? Why?
4. Is there anything that you would do differently if you were to do this project again? What? Why?

Questions 3 and 4 are a way of evaluating your project. Evaluation is important if we are to learn from our past learning, or our mistakes, and make more progress in the future.

Secure

1. How did you make visible the data to track the health of the local commons over time?
2. How did you measure the progress of your project?
3. How did you involve and educate the community about your project?

If there is time, answer the questions from 'Developing' too.

Extending

Answer the questions for 'Secure' and the questions below.

1. How did you work with a local government agency or community-based organization to improve the way we measure the health of our commons? What happened as a result?
2. How did you include the most appropriate ways of evaluating the health of the commons in your plan?
3. Which local government office or community-based organization did you ask for a review and input on your plan? What happened as a result of that input?
4. How have you created a way that continues to communicate about your project over time?

Work individually and write all your answers in your Project Notebook.

Setting goals

Although your project is finished, your ability to learn about tracking the health of a local commons continues!

In your Project Notebook, write down some short-, medium-, and long-term goals for yourself, to make sure you keep learning. Below are some examples to get you thinking.

Short-term goal:

Example: For the next four weeks, I will continue to measure the progress of my project. I will also continue to involve and educate the community about what I have done.

____

____

Medium-term goal:

Example: By the end of this year, I will have reflected on the success of this project and thought about another project in which I want to help to protect another local commons.

____

____

Long-term goal:

Example: By the time I am 20, I want to have inspired at least ten other people to have developed their own project to protect or improve the health of one of their local commons. I will advise them about what to do.

____

____

Think about what you need to do to complete this, and work hard to do it! And finally, try to do something positive for Earth every day!

3 Turning problems into opportunities

Contents

Dear Student,

You have reached your final project of Year 9! In this project we challenge you to create a solution to an 'upstream' problem within your sphere of influence. This solution will help us move towards a sustainable future.

In this project, you will identify the difference between problems and symptoms. This is an important skill. Finding the most 'upstream' problem you can work on within your sphere of influence will:

- solve more than one problem/symptom at a time

- minimize new problems.

This will set us on the way to the future we want: a healthy and sustainable future for all! You will identify local symptoms and investigate the 'upstream' problems behind them.

Mindsets are often the most 'upstream' place we can change. You will:

- describe the mindsets that will help us to make the shift towards sustainability

- assess your use of them

- determine the strategies you will use to develop those mindsets over time, in order to reach your goals.

You will work in small groups to identify an 'upstream' challenge in your area that is:

- within your sphere of influence

- that needs to be addressed so we can move toward a sustainable future.

You will then plan and implement a solution that yields helpful outcomes. What a great opportunity this will be to make positive changes in your area!

Finally, you will reflect on your experience of working together to achieve a goal. You will consider the skills that you needed to do this, and you will teach others what you have learned.

Enjoy this opportunity. Have fun exploring and working on your project!

Best wishes,

The Sustainability Team

The consequences of treating the symptom

You have studied problems and symptoms before. In Year 7, you learned that a symptom is a sign, or an indicator, that there is a problem. The symptom is caused by that underlying problem.

Think back to a game that you played in Year 7. The object of the game was that when the music stopped, you had to take a seat. The teacher took a chair away each time, and those people without a chair were out of the game. In this game, we could say that the symptom was: I/we need a place to sit.

Once the chairs started disappearing, what strategies did you use to find somewhere to sit? Discuss these as a class. Those strategies probably seemed to work for a while.

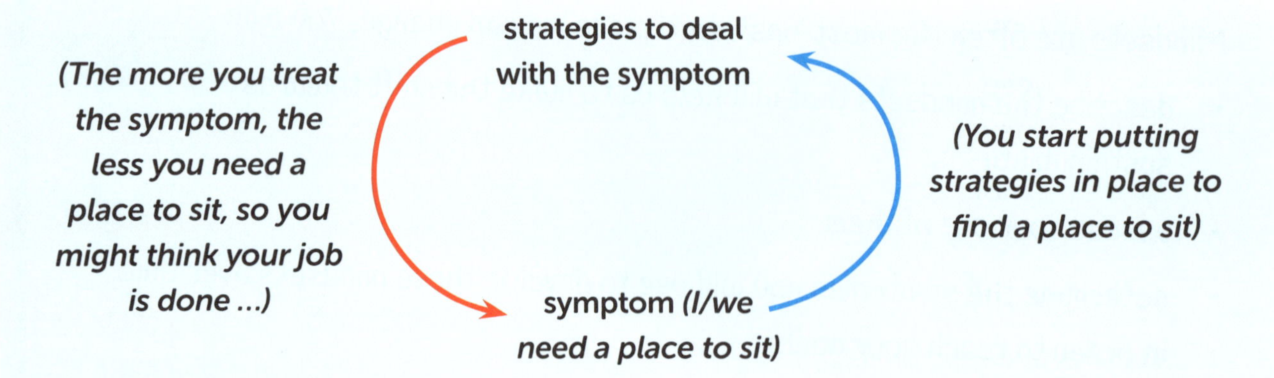

But what happened over time?

The source of the problem was that there were fewer and fewer chairs.

If we treat the symptom and not the source, then over time there will be unintended consequences that make it harder and harder to treat the symptom, and we create new problems!

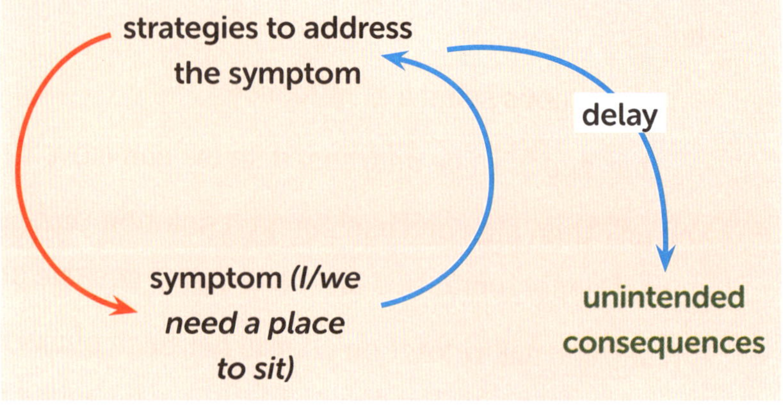

Let's get talking

With a partner, briefly discuss a headache as an example of a symptom.

- What strategies could you use to address that symptom?
- What might be unintended consequences of only addressing the symptom of the headache?

Then share your ideas as a class.

Treating the upstream problem

In Year 7, you learned that the upstream problem is the same as the underlying problem behind the symptoms.

In the game example, the upstream problem was: the number of chairs was decreasing.

Ways of dealing with the upstream problem included:

- students decided not to leave their seats

- talking to the teacher and asking them not to take the chair away

- stopping the music from playing so that the teacher cannot play the game.

What are the results of tackling the upstream problem rather than the symptom? For example:

- The more we protect the resources, the fewer chairs disappear. The fewer chairs that disappear, the less effort you need to find a place to sit.

- The less you need to find a place to sit, the fewer strategies you need to use to find somewhere to sit.

- Now, we have more time and energy for other things, your clothes aren't as dirty because you aren't sitting on the floor, and so on.

By addressing the upstream problem, you have:

- contributed towards solving more than one problem at a time

and

- minimized new problems developing.

Some examples of symptoms and upstream problems have been included on the activity on page 99–100.

This algal bloom on the surface of a lake is a
symptom of an underlying problem.

Identifying local challenges and their symptoms

Look at the pictures below, which are examples of possible local issues.
Are they problems or symptoms? Discuss as a class.

Litter

Homelessness

Poor health

Pollution

Consider what local symptoms there are in your community.

Do the following in pairs or small groups:

1. List a range of symptoms in your local community.

2. Research what the upstream problems are (or might be) for each of
    those symptoms.

Write your answers in your Project Notebook.

Once you have finished, share your ideas with the class.

Linking the symptom to the upstream challenge

Our most important action should be to address the upstream problems that are within our sphere of influence. This means the problems that we can do something about! You learned in Lesson 1 that by addressing the upstream problem, we solve more than one problem at a time, and we minimize new problems developing. We must make sure we have found the upstream problem before we can deal with it and solve the symptoms too.

To check that you have found the upstream problem to each of your symptoms, create one or more flow diagrams.

Start with the symptom. Show what causes each step, until you reach the upstream problem. One possible example is shown below. There are, of course, other reasons why people drop litter. You should explore what is correct for your area.

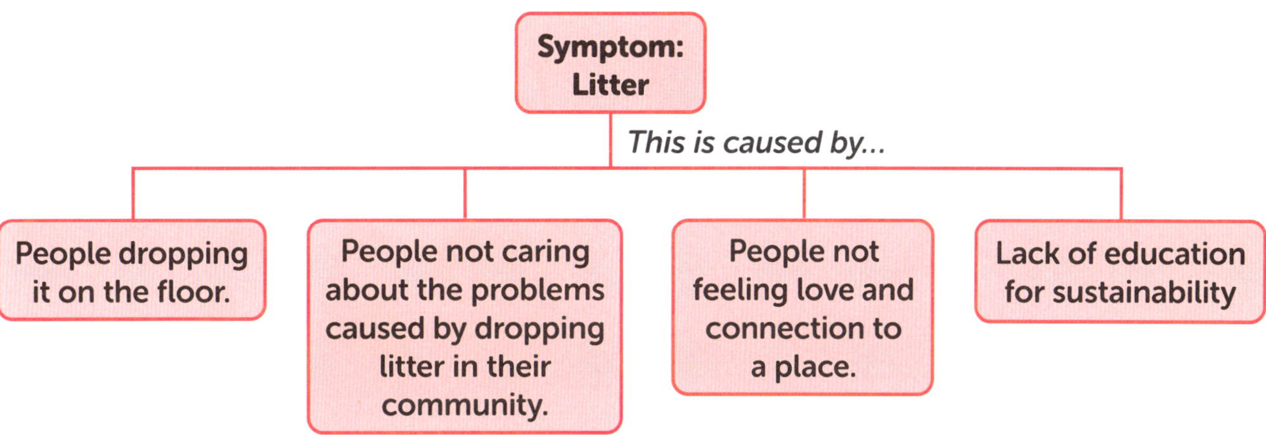

Solution to upstream problem: We need clear educational programmes in schools to teach people about the benefits of loving and caring for the community

In your Project Notebook, draw your own flow diagrams similar to the one above. Start with the symptom and work through each step until you get to the upstream problem. You may find that several symptoms have the same upstream problem.

Write a short paragraph to explain why it is important to identify the upstream problem. Use your own words. Include an example from this lesson to explain your point.

Mindsets for sustainability

Take a moment to remember all the mindsets of sustainability and unsustainability you have studied before. They are written on the activity on page 101–102. For example:

Greed

We Are All Responsible

The Controller

Practical Idealist

On your activity, highlight the mindsets which will help us make the shift towards sustainability. (Leave the boxes that say 'Example' blank for now.)

In your Project Notebook, describe how each of the mindsets you have chosen will help us to move towards sustainability.

In Year 7, you considered which mindsets you had about global warming and climate change. Are these still the same? Or have they changed since Year 7? If your mindset has changed, how do you think that has that affected your behaviour?

Which mindsets do you use?

Which mindsets do you have about other issues? Consider all the parts of sustainability:

- the economy
- society
- the environment.

On your activity, tick those mindsets which you use.

For example:

Do you buy **biodegradable** products? Or support local produce? (Live by the Natural Laws, **Reciprocity**, We are All Responsible for the Difference we Make)

Do you feel left out if you don't have a device that your friends have, even though the device wasn't sustainably produced? (Social Trap)

Do you volunteer in your local community? (We are All in this Together)

Do you dream of making lots of money and living in a big house? Does it matter to you how you make that money? (Maximizing **Gains** for Self)

Underneath each of the mindsets you have chosen, give an example of when or why you use that mindset.

Let's get talking

In pairs, discuss the following questions to consider what you have found out and what your next steps should be.

- To what extent are you using mindsets that will help us make the shift towards sustainability?
- Which mindsets are you using that will not help us make the shift towards sustainability?
- Which mindsets are you most proud about using? Why?
- If you notice that you have been using unsustainable mindsets, what could happen if you shifted to a sustainable mindset? What difference could that make?
- To what extent do you want to change some of the mindsets you are using?
- How will you change those mindsets?

Now discuss your answers as a class.

Identifying the goal, the challenges, and the solutions

In Lesson 2, you identified some upstream challenges in your local area. Over the next five lessons, you are going to implement solutions to those challenges.

First, we will think about the following questions:

- How have other young people found solutions to upstream challenges?

- How have those solutions led to many different positive outcomes?

Watch the video your teacher shows you. As you are watching, answer the questions on the activity on page 103. Discuss your answers as a class.

Remember, to implement any solution effectively, it is important to do the following:

1   Identify the goal. You have learned before that by having a vision for the future, we can bring what we care about into existence.

2   Identify the upstream challenge that needs to be addressed so you can reach your goal. You must find the challenge before you can solve it!

3   Identify strategies that will solve the challenge and create more than one positive outcome for your goal.

Yielding positive outcomes

You have learned that addressing the upstream challenge:

*   contributes towards solving more than one problem at a time

*   minimizes the development of new problems.

So, how do you implement a solution which addresses an upstream challenge and yields many positive outcomes?

Do the following tasks in small groups:

1. Identify the goal or goals that you want to achieve.

2. Identify one or more challenges that you will need to address in order to achieve your goal.

3. Now choose one upstream challenge that your group wants to focus on.

This can be the same or a different challenge that you have tackled before. If you are choosing the same challenge, make sure you are building on (or improving) your previous work to make this a meaningful project.

Remember that a challenge may not always be about solving a problem. You may choose to preserve or protect something as well.

What were the upstream challenges that you identified in Lesson 2? You can choose one of those or choose a new one. For example:

Are the changes due to global warming causing a local water source to dry up?

Do people need more education to learn and change their ways?

4. Think of a strategy, or strategies, within your sphere of influence that you can use to address the challenge and achieve the goal. For example:

    *   Do you need to educate people through talks, posters, campaigns, or other information?

    *   Do you need to contact your local government and ask for action?

    *   What else could you do?

5. Identify the positive outcomes that will be achieved with your solution.

Write your ideas on a large piece of paper, then circle the ones you like the best.

Planning how to implement the solution

In Lesson 4, you identified:

- the goal or goals to achieve

- one upstream challenge within your sphere of influence that your group wants to address

- strategies to tackle that challenge and achieve the goal

- the positive outcomes that will be achieved.

Now, work as a group to create a detailed plan. This plan will be about how you are going to implement your solution. Remember all the things you have learned before about how to run a project like this. For example:

- how to evaluate solutions to consider which might be the best

- how to start with baseline data and how to track your progress to make sure you are progressing toward your goal

- how to create a campaign (if that is relevant to your solution)

- how to generate questions that need to be addressed before writing your plan

- how to be a responsible, productive, and creative project collaborator

- how you will contribute most effectively to the project.

Let's get talking

Remember what sorts of questions you have asked before when making a plan such as this. For example, discuss the following:

- What are the different steps we need to take to achieve our end goal?
- What questions do we need to answer before we start? (e.g. who makes decisions about what we are trying to protect? How much money is needed to do what we want to do?)
- What specific tasks need to be done and who will do them?
- How long will each task take?
- Are there any specific dates we need to keep in mind (e.g. town meetings)?
- What dates do we need to have completed each task by?
- Are there any other options for the solutions? Which one is most suitable and why?
- How do we keep ourselves, and others, safe as we are implementing our plans?
- How are we going to monitor and assess our progress?

Then write your plan in your Project Notebook or using the activity on page 104–106.

Peer-mark your plans

When you have finished your plan, swap it with another group. Read the other group's plan and give them feedback.

When giving feedback, think about the following questions, and anything else that might be relevant:

1. Will the solution they are suggesting help them achieve their goal?

   The solution may not solve the whole challenge, but it should make a good contribution. For example, Milo didn't stop all restaurants from providing plastic straws, but his campaign had a significant impact.

2. Will the solution yield more than one positive outcome? Are they listed?

3. Is it clear how they will implement the solution?

4. Have they missed out any steps which you think are important?

5. Is there any other information that they should consider further?

6. Have they clearly planned how to minimize risk to themselves and others?

Remember that your classmates will have worked hard on their plans. Deliver your feedback with kindness and tact. Value the work that they have done and empathize if a mistake has been made. Be clear and honest about:

- what they have done well
- what they still need to do to improve.

Now, revisit your own plan. Are there any changes you need to make, based on the feedback you have received?

Take the opportunity to make those changes.

Starting to implement your solution

In Lesson 5, you wrote a plan for achieving a goal by addressing an upstream challenge.

Before you do anything else, you must get your plans checked by your teacher before you start to implement any solution.

Once you have had your plans checked, start following the steps that you have planned. For example, the boy in the Be Straw Free campaign:

- visited restaurants to persuade them not to give out plastic straws to everyone, or to use more sustainable straws instead

- created a website to spread his message

- talked to local, national, and international media, and made presentations to people in charge.

Make sure that everyone in your group is completing a specific task to help you implement your solution.

Overcoming obstacles

When you are implementing your solution, you will probably come across some obstacles, or events not going quite as planned.

For example:

- People within your group may disagree about what to do.

- A meeting that you were planning to speak at may not happen.
- People that you are trying to persuade may not immediately seem very excited or interested in your ideas.

Discuss how you might get around obstacles such as these.

What other possible obstacles can you think of that you might have to face?

As a class, quickly discuss how you could deal with these and still reach your goal.

Remember that any possible problem gives you the opportunity to be creative and think of an alternative strategy. Your current strategies may only need changing slightly to work next time.

You will use Lesson 7 and 8 to continue to implement your solutions. You may also need to carry out some actions in your own time outside of school. Tell your teacher what you are planning to do. Make sure your teacher has confirmed your plans are okay before you carry out any actions outside of school.

Monitoring your progress

In this lesson, you are going to continue to implement your solution to an upstream challenge.

As part of your project, continue to monitor your progress. This involves the following:

- Knowing what the starting point was. (This may involve baseline data.)

- Knowing what your end point will be.

- Being able to measure what progress you have made towards achieving your goal. This information will be different for every project. For example, it might involve:

Recording how many people visit your website.

Knowing how many businesses have changed their practices because of your actions.

Using questionnaires to see how mindsets have changed since you started.

Monitoring species in an ecosystem.

Use the following questions to start to consider how you will monitor your progress.

- How do you know what your starting point is?

- How do you know what your end point is?

- How will you monitor your progress throughout your project

Continue to implement your solution. Keep monitoring your progress and record the information in your Project Notebook.

Evaluating your work so far

Reflect on your progress so far.

Answer the questions below in your Project Notebook. This evaluation will help you to continue to progress to the next lesson. When you are evaluating your work, think about how well you are working as a team as well as how effectively you are carrying out your plan.

1. What is working well so far?

2. What is not working so well?

3. Why are these things not working so well?

4. What changes (if any) do you need to make so that your work can progress effectively in the next lesson?

Use your superpowers!

As you continue to implement your solutions, remember your work from previous years.

In Year 7, you learned that your 'superpowers' mean you can make a unique contribution to a project.

What are your superpowers? For example:

- Can you do detailed research to find out the best way to preserve a local ecosystem?

- Can you make sure that everyone on your team manages their time effectively?

- Or can you do something else?

In Year 8, you created performance criteria to describe a responsible, productive, and creative project collaborator.

Use your superpowers and those criteria that you created now. Make sure that you are being a responsible, productive, and creative project collaborator as you implement your solution.

Finish implementing your solution

Use the remainder of this lesson to continue to implement your solution.

Although you will be doing other work in the next few lessons, continue to implement your solution at home until you have made significant progress on addressing your upstream challenge. Make sure you have checked what you intend to do with your teacher. You will have the chance to evaluate your project in Lesson 11.

Near the end of the lesson, use these questions to decide on the next steps for your group.

- What have you achieved so far?
- What still needs to be done to implement your solution?
- Who will do what, and by when?

If you are aiming for 'Extending', use a causal loop diagram to explain what you have done in your project. Here is an example of a simple causal loop diagram about the Be Straw Free campaign.

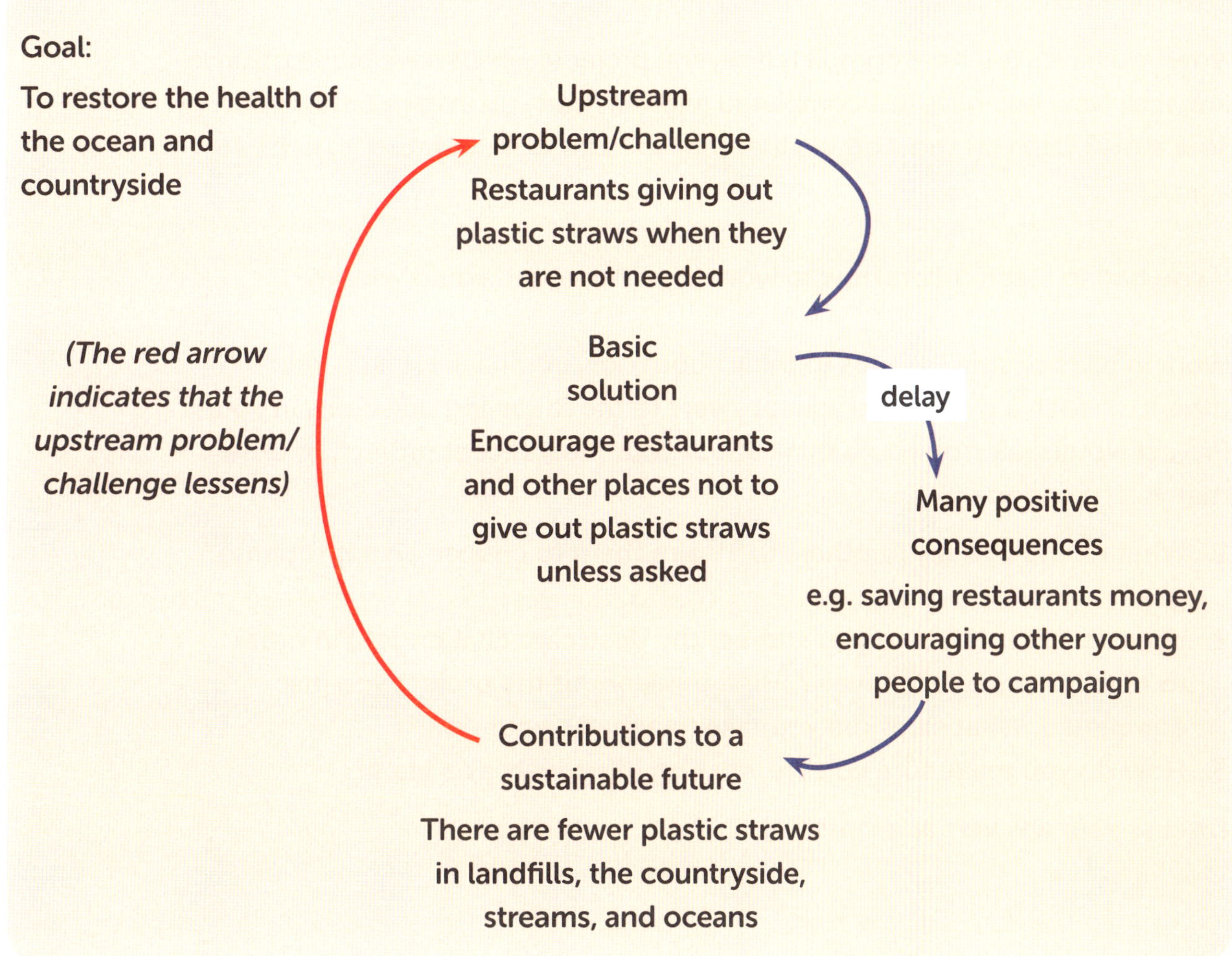

How do you work together?

Think back to all the case studies you have looked at of young people making positive impacts in their communities and around the world. For example:

- How some students from Pakistan helped to deal with heat waves (Year 8, Project 1).

- How a group of students campaigned for solar power in their town, and saved a local forest from being cut down (Year 9, Project 2).

- How a boy called Milo campaigned against using plastic straws (Year 9, Project 3).

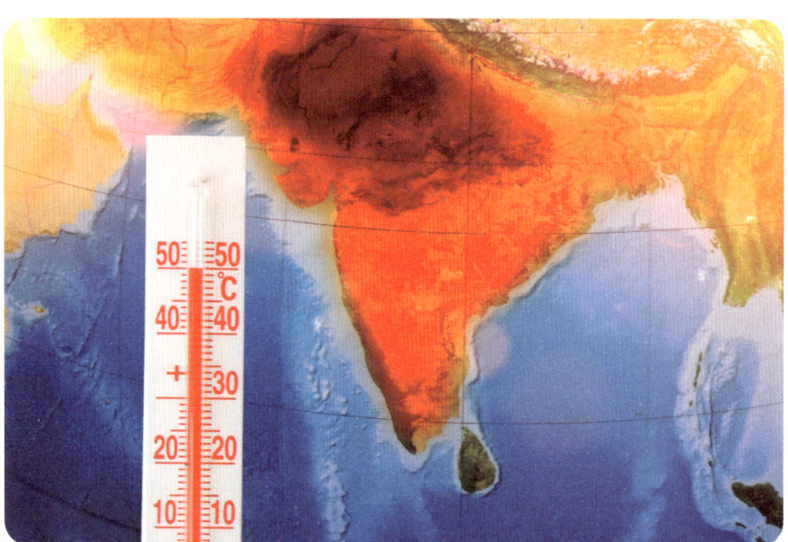

How did hearing their stories make you feel? Did you feel inspired to make a positive impact yourself?

Now you have! You have completed several projects which have made positive impacts. Now you have just completed another. Can you inspire others with your story? Can you show others that they too can work together to achieve a goal?

If you had to teach others how to work together, what would you say?

Work in pairs or small groups to think about how you have worked with others to reach a goal. Write your answers to the following questions in your Project Notebook. You could think about your most recent project, or others that you have done.

1. What would you say to others to inspire them to choose an appropriate goal?
2. How do you make sure you address the upstream challenge(s) in order to reach the goal effectively? (Hint: think about the project you just completed. What steps did you take to achieve your goal?)
3. How do you make sure you are working effectively as a team?

Discuss your answers as a class.

What is the best way to teach others?

How can you now teach that information to others?

Here are some ideas:

- Perform a drama sketch to demonstrate what you know.

- Deliver a presentation or assembly.

- Create an information sheet, poster, or website.

What other ways could you choose to inspire others and teach them how to work together to achieve a goal? The method you choose might change depending on who you are teaching.

As a class, discuss who you will be teaching. For example, you could teach:

Other students in your class

Students in other classes or the whole school

Your family

Other people in your community

In pairs or small groups, discuss different ways that you could teach those people. Decide which method is the best.

Start to prepare what you need to deliver your chosen teaching method. For example, plan the drama sketch, write the presentation, or create the information sheet. You will have the rest of this lesson and the beginning of next lesson to complete this task.

Teaching others

The learning objective for this lesson is to teach others how to work together to achieve a goal.

In your pairs or small groups, do the following tasks:

1. Finish preparing everything you need to teach others. (This is the work you started in Lesson 9.)

2. Practise and check what you are going to do. For example:

Practise the presentation.

Check the information sheet, poster, or website for mistakes.

If you are planning to teach people outside of your class, you will need to do this in your own time. Check your plans with your teacher to make sure you keep yourself and others safe. Then, in lesson time, practise teaching others by presenting your work to your classmates first.

Local actions and global consequences

After you have taught others, reflect on the impact that your local actions can, and will, have.

You have learned about others' stories. These are from countries including Pakistan and the USA. There are many more examples from around the world.

The lessons that you have taught others can, and will, spread to other people – and maybe to other countries too!

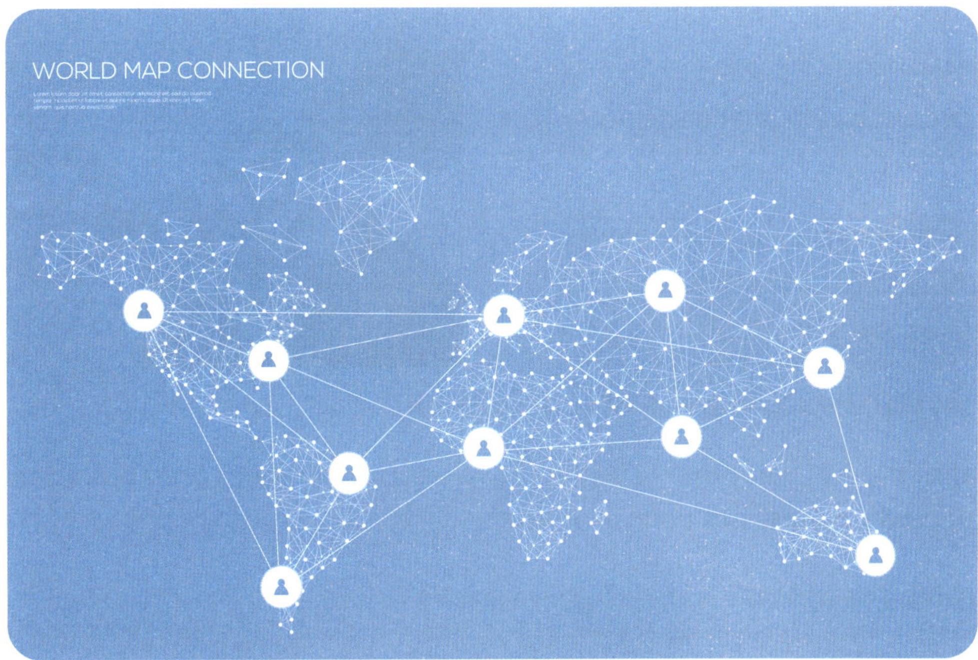

Consider how your local actions might have global impacts.

Evaluating your solution

Since Lesson 8, you have continued to implement your solutions to an upstream challenge. It may be that this work is now complete, or you may still have opportunities to develop your work further. Whatever stage you are at, reflect on what you have achieved.

Evaluation is a key part of any project. It means you can reflect on:

- what went well
- what could be improved if you did a similar project again in the future.

Remember, when you are evaluating your project, there are lots of different parts of the project to consider. For example:

- the goal you are working towards
- the solution to the upstream challenge you focused on

Was it the right solution? Was it within your sphere of influence? Did it solve the upstream problem as you intended?

- the strategies that you used to implement your solution

Were they all as effective as each other? Did you have enough time to complete them? Were there unexpected obstacles to your progress?

- how well you worked as a team

Did you all contribute the same amount? Were you all clear what your tasks were, and did you carry them out effectively?

- the processes that you used to monitor progress.

Did you know how well you were making progress?

Let's get talking

Discuss the questions with your project group:

- To what extent have you been able contribute to the achievement of your goal and solve an upstream challenge?
- Which part of your project was the most successful, and why?
- Which part of your project was the least successful, and why?
- What were the multiple positive outcomes from your project?

Then write detailed answers to the questions in your Project Notebook, or on the activity on page 107. Include examples from your project to support your answers.

Let's celebrate!

Think back to all the things you have done in this project:

1. You have identified the difference between problems and symptoms, and identified upstream problems in your area.

2. You have described the mindsets that will help us move towards sustainability. You have assessed your own use of them.

3. You have identified an upstream challenge. You have implemented a solution that yields many positive outcomes.

4. You have taught others how to work together to reach a goal.

In your Project Notebook, write down what you are most proud of about your work for each of the learning objectives. Don't be embarrassed to share your achievements!

What about other people in your class? Who has impressed you? Whose achievements should you celebrate? For example, maybe they have:

- implemented a really effective solution to an upstream problem

- worked outside of their normal comfort zone to contribute to the team effort

- been honest about their mindsets and already taken steps to make positive changes

- taught a wide range of people about how to work together to achieve a goal.

Work with a partner to design a certificate to recognize your classmates' achievements. Then hand out the certificates to your peers. Be proud of everything you have done!

A reflection of the year

Think about everything you have done this year.

Project 1: Thriving on Earth

- Advocated for why people should understand nature's laws and principles.
- Understood that healthy systems live within the biological capacity and resource replenishment rates.
- Created a campaign to protect and restore the health of the ecosystem services that we depend on.
- Described a day in your future life in which everything you do contributes to your health and the health of our Earth.

Project 2: Tracking the health of a local commons

- Collected and made visible data to track the health of a local commons over time.
- Evaluated some ways in which we can protect or improve the health of our community.
- Wrote a plan to care for a local commons that we depend on and are responsible for.
- Developed, implemented, and measured the progress of a community plan that involves and educates the community.

Project 3: Turning problems into opportunities

- Identified the difference between problems and symptoms (problem finding before problem solving).
- Described the mindsets that will help us make the shift towards sustainability, and assessed your own use of them.
- Identified an 'upstream' challenge and implemented a solution that yields positive outcomes.
- Taught others how to work together to achieve a goal.

Let's get talking

In your Project Notebook, answer the questions about all three projects combined.

- **What are you most proud of in this year?**
- **What skills do you think you developed?**
- **What was the most interesting thing that you learned?**
- **What was the most useful thing that you learned?**

Then discuss your answers as a class.

Setting goals

Although your project is finished, your ability to learn about creating an upstream solution continues!

In your Project Notebook, write down some short-, medium-, and long-term goals for yourself, to make sure you keep learning. Make these goals specific to the work you did in Project 3.

Short-term goal:

Example: In the next two weeks, I will continue to take the actions needed to implement our solution to address the upstream challenge and deliver impacts.

____

____

Medium-term goal:

Example: The next time I see a symptom, I will work out the upstream problem and take steps to tackle that problem.

____

____

Long-term goal:

Example: I will continue to assess my mindsets and be honest with myself. I will continue to work hard to use mindsets which will help us make the shift towards sustainability.

____

____

Think about what you need to do to carry these goals out, and work hard to do it! And finally, try to do something positive for Earth every day!

How does nature behave?

1. Look at the building below. It is more than 600 years old. Predict what it would look like if it was abandoned for 80 years.

My prediction

2. This building is around the same age as the building in the first picture. It was abandoned in the 1940s.

a) Draw or describe what has happened to the building.

b) How close was your prediction about the first building?

c) How has nature behaved in the example of the second building?

d) From this example, what do you understand about how nature behaves everywhere in the world?

How are ecosystem services in danger?

Complete the table to explain how the health of some ecosystem services is at risk from human activity. Make sure you refer to specific ecosystem services in your explanations.

	Explain how human behaviour could harm ecosystem services.

How else is human behaviour harming ecosystem services? Explain your ideas below.

Use the flow diagram below to test your idea from page 19 of the Project Book.

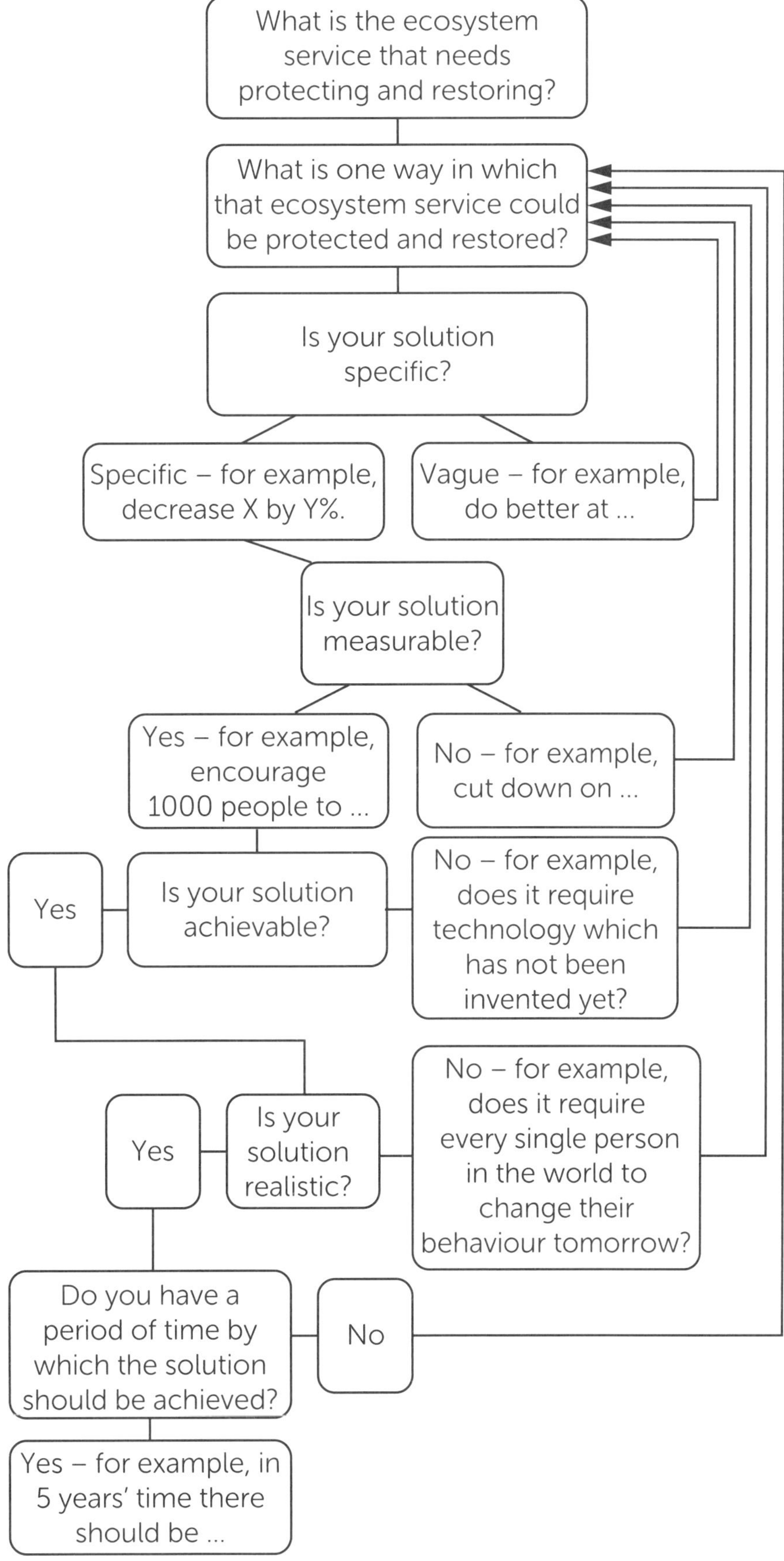

Planning your campaign

Plan your campaign by answering these questions.

Campaign aims

1. What is the aim of your campaign? Think about your solutions from Lesson 6 and keep this aim as SMART as possible.

2. Which ecosystem service(s) does your campaign aim to protect and restore to health?

3. What exactly do you want other people to do or to learn? How do you want behaviours to change? Keep it simple.

Bringing about change

4. How are you going to share your message most effectively? Which method(s) are you going to use in your campaign? Think back to the list you wrote in your Project Notebook.

5. What resources will you need? For example, will you need a computer or paper, or something else?

6. How long will it take you to create your campaign? Will you need help from anyone else?

7. Add in more details about your campaign. For example:

    *   How often do you need to send out your message?
    *   Where will you post your information?
    *   How are you going to make sure that other people care about your message?
    *   How are you going to make sure people don't forget the message?

Imagining your future life

What will your life look like in 20 years' time?

Use the boxes below to write down what you imagine or hope for.

Home

First ideas

Second ideas

Job

First ideas

Second ideas

Transport

First ideas

Second ideas

Leisure time

First ideas

Second ideas

Food and drink

First ideas

Second ideas

Any other information

First ideas

Second ideas

Your local commons

1. Complete the second column of the table. Use your own knowledge or a map of your local area.
2. Complete the third column of the table. Do this by:
   - considering what might show the health of that commons
   - choosing an indicator or indicators that would measure that health.

Type of commons	Named example in your local area	Indicators to measure its health
Playgrounds, parks, and other green spaces		
Public transport		
Education and learning		
Local wildlife		

Local history and culture		
Source of water		
Places to improve public health		
Places of government, or law enforcement		
Streets and pavements		
Sources of food or energy		

Data collection methods

Answer the questions in your Project Notebook.

1. Which local commons do you want to protect?

2. Which indicator will you use to track the health of that commons?

3. How will you collect data to track the health of that commons?
   a) What data do you need to collect?

   b) Where will you collect that data? Be specific (e.g. name the places you will collect the data, or which websites you will use).

   c) How much data do you need to collect? (e.g. How many questionnaires will you ask? How long will you do the count for? How many times?)

   d) Who will collect which pieces of data?

   e) Add in any other information about how you will collect the data.

4. Which sampling strategy will you use and why?

5. How will you continue to track your data over time? How often will you need to collect your data in the future? Who will do that and when?

Data collection

Part 1 – Staying safe

1. Copy the table into your Project Notebook, extending it to list the risks you might face while collecting your data.

2. Once you have discussed your answers as a class, write down how you could minimize those risks.

Possible risk	How to minimize that risk

Part 2 – Wildlife count

Copy the tally chart into your Project Notebook, allowing lots of space for your tallies. Use it to tally your wildlife count.

Type of wildlife	Tally	Total
Birds		
Insects		
Other wildlife		

Improving the health of your community

Answer the questions in your Project Notebook.

1. Choose five different ways of protecting or improving the health of our community, and write them in a table like this.

Method	Rating from 1–5

2. Evaluate each method. Rate each one on a scale from 1–5 (5 being the most effective). Use the criteria that you discussed as a class to do your evaluations.

3. Complete these statements.

   a) The most effective method is:

   b) This method is the most effective because:

   c) The least effective method is:

   d) This method is the least effective because:

Your method

Complete the statements below.
The aim of our project was to:

To achieve this aim, we implemented our plan.
First, we:

We did this because:

Second, we:

We did this because:

Third, we:

We did this because:

Results and conclusion

1. Are things better, the same, or worse than they were before?

2. How do you know?

3. Have you achieved your end goal?

4. How do you know?

5. If you haven't achieved your end goal yet, what progress have you made?

6. What do you still need to do, to make sure you achieve your end goal?

Considering the benefits of problem-finding

What happens when we treat the symptom on the way to a goal? What happens when we treat the upstream problem instead?

Complete the table to show your understanding of addressing symptoms and problems on the way to achieving a goal.

1. Add at least one suggestion in each box in the table. Add more if you can.

- Remove the algae from the pond
- Take painkillers
- Go to bed early enough to get a good rest
- Educate people about the benefits of loving and caring for your community
- The classroom becomes cold
- The painkillers cost money
- Build a sea wall to protect against flooding
- Drink plenty of water
- It takes time and energy to remove the algae
- Stop burning fossil fuels
- Have the window wide open to try to stay awake
- Pick the litter up
- Fine the business to stop it from releasing the pollutants into the water
- The sea wall is very expensive
- People think that others are picking it up so they keep dropping more

2. In your own words, explain why it is important to treat the upstream problem (the source) and not the symptom.

Goal	Symptom	Strategies to solve the symptom	Unintended consequences	Upstream problem (the source)	Strategies to address the problem (which lead to multiple positive outcomes)
Good health	Headache			Not drinking enough water	
High achievement at school	Can't concentrate at school			Didn't get enough sleep the night before	
A clean neighbourhood	Litter			Lack of love and connection to a place	
A healthy lake	A lake has lots of algae			A local business is releasing pollutants into the water	
A sustainable future	Climate change			Global warming	

Mindsets for sustainability

Maximizing Gains for Self (making the gains for yourself as big as possible) – "I put myself first before others."	**Live by the Natural Laws** – We must live within our planet's physical laws and ecological principles.	**Reciprocity** – Self-interests are best achieved through mutually beneficial relationships (relationships that have positive outcomes for all parties).
Example:	**Example:**	**Example:**
Healthy Systems have Limits – Use the power of limits rather than exceed or ignore them. Limits inspire creativity.	**It's Only a Game** – "Let's just play and see what happens."	**Practical** Idealist – "A healthy and sustainable future is possible. We can do it!"
Example:	**Example:**	**Example:**
Greed – "I want a lot and I don't care about the consequences."	**There's Nothing We Can Do** – "Things are the way they are and there's nothing I/we can do about it."	**Zero-Sum Game** – "You can either win or lose. I am not a loser; I play to win." People think that winning and losing are the only options.
Example:	**Example:**	**Example:**

We are All Responsible – Everything we do and everything we don't do makes a difference.	The Titanic – "If I'm going down anyway, I might as well go down first class." If people think there aren't enough resources available, they assume scarcity and will hoard.	Everything is Substitutable – "If we run out of this, that's okay; we will just find another thing to replace it."
Example:	Example:	Example:
We are All in This Together – We depend on each other and Earth's natural systems.	Anthropocentric (thinking that people are the most important things in the universe) – "I was thinking about myself and other people. I didn't think about nature."	Theory of Confidence – "Someone, or something, else will take care of it."
Example:	Example:	Example:
The Controller – "I am in control. Everyone must do as I say."	Social Trap – "If others do it, I may as well ... If no one else does it, why should I?"	
Example:	Example:	

Source: The Cloud Institute for Sustainability Education

Be Straw Free campaign

1. What was Milo's goal?

2. What was the symptom Milo identified?

3. What was the upstream challenge behind that symptom?

4. What strategies did he use to address that challenge?

5. How did his campaign lead to many positive outcomes? (Think of lots of different benefits that his actions created.)

Your plan

The end goal that we want to achieve is:

The upstream challenge our group wants to address is:

The strategies we will use to address the challenge are:

Solving this upstream challenge will yield the following positive outcomes:

It will yield these positive outcomes by:

Questions we need to answer before we start are:

____

____

____

____

____

The steps we need to take to achieve our end goal are:

Task	Who will do the task	Date to achieve the task by

Activity page for Lesson 5 (page 68)

We will monitor and measure progress by:

____

____

____

We will know we have been successful by:

____

____

Staying safe

Possible risk	How to minimize that risk

Evaluating your solution

1. Did you contribute to achieving your goal and solving the upstream challenge?

2. Which part of your project was the most successful?

3. Give at least two reasons why this part of the project was successful.

4. Which part of your project was the least successful?

5. Give at least two reasons why this part of the project was the least successful.

6. List three or more positive outcomes from your project.

Word bank

abandon: to leave and never return to something

activist: a person who works to bring about political or social change

address: to think about a problem or a situation and decide how you are going to deal with it

advocate: to support something in public; you say why you think something is important and why you support it

affordable: cheap enough that people can afford to pay it or buy it

annotate: to add labels with explanations or comments

baseline data: a set of information that is the starting point for a research project

biodegradable: can be changed or broken down to a natural state that will not harm the environment

biological capacity: the ability of an ecosystem to produce useful resources and deal with waste

campaign: (noun) planned series of actions that are designed to achieve a particular goal

campaign: (verb) to take part in activities to try and achieve change

carrying capacity: the maximum size of a population in an area which is determined by the area's resources and what those resources can support

causal loop diagram: a type of diagram that explains or shows complex connections

comfort zone: a place or situation in which you feel safe or comfortable

commons: things that we share and look after, such as the air, climate, oceans, languages, and cultures; we all have rights to them, and we all have responsibilities to take care of them over time

contribute: to give something to help achieve or provide something

contribution: an action or a service that helps to cause or increase something, often something good or valuable

coral reef: coral is formed from the bones of very small sea creatures; a coral reef is a long line of coral that forms an ocean habitat

count: an act of counting to find the total number of somebody/something

criteria: standards we can use to decide on something

data: facts or information collected through research

decay: the process or result of being destroyed by natural causes or by not being cared for

demonstrate: to show by your actions that you have a particular quality, feeling, or opinion

desertification: when land is turning into desert because the soil is losing its fertility

diversity: a range of many people or things that are very different from each other

drought: a long period of time when there is little or no rain

ecological footprint: how much of Earth's resources you are using to support your lifestyle

ecological succession: the process by which the mix of species and habitat in an area changes over time

ecosystem service: a service that we get from nature

empathize: to understand another person's feelings and experiences

enhance: improve the quality or value of something

entropy: a scientific idea that describes the amount of disorder in a system, and how much energy is needed to maintain a system

evaluate: to form an opinion of the amount, value, or quality of something after thinking about it carefully

evaluation: the process of forming an opinion about something after thinking about it carefully

existence: the state or fact of being real or living or of being present

fertility: the quality in land or soil of making plants grow well

field sketch: a drawing made while you are out doing practical work

fossil fuels: natural fuels containing hydrogen and carbon, such as coal, oil, and natural gas, formed from living organisms that died a long time ago

gain: an advantage or improvement

generate: to produce or create something

greed: wanting more money, possessions, power, etc. than you need

greenhouse gases: gases found in Earth's atmosphere that trap heat

idealist: a person who believes that a perfect life, situation, etc. can be achieved, even when this is not very likely

implement: to put something, like a plan, into action

index: a sign or measure that something can be judged by

indicator: a sign that helps us to measure the health of something or to measure progress

infertile: when the quality of the soil on a piece of land becomes so poor that it cannot produce good crops or vegetation

key: an explanation of the symbols used on a map or plan

living system: a system in which living things work together and affect one another and their environment; they include cells, plants, people, schools, and communities; the different parts of the system are connected, and they make patterns and relationships

maximize: to increase something as much as possible

meaningful: important and useful

mindset: a set of attitudes or fixed ideas that somebody has and that are often difficult to change

minimize: to reduce something, especially something bad, to the lowest possible level

natural limits: things that we cannot do or change, even with the use of technology

obstacle: a situation, an event, etc. that makes it difficult for you to do or achieve something

outcome: result

overcultivation: growing too many crops, which reduces the ability of the soil to grow more

overgrazing: when animals like cows and sheep are allowed to eat too much grass or too many plants in a specific place

peer: a person who is the same age as you

peer-mark: when someone who is the same age as you marks your work, instead of your teacher

performance criteria: standards we can use to decide on how well something or someone is working

pesticide: a chemical used for killing insects or animals that destroy plants

petition: a document signed by many people calling for change

pollutant: a substance that makes something dirty or unhealthy, especially air and water

preserve: to keep something in good condition

primary data: information taken directly from a data source

principle: any idea or belief that influences the way you act and behave

questionnaire: a written list of questions that are answered by a number of people so that information can be collected from the answers

rating: a measurement of how good, popular, important, etc. somebody/ something is, especially in relation to other people or things

reciprocity: a situation in which two people, countries, etc. provide the same or similar help or advantages to each other

resource replenishment rate: how quickly and effectively an ecosystem can replace its resources

restore: to bring something back to its previous condition

sampling: the process of taking an example set of information

secondary data: data collected by someone else, but available for others to use

soil erosion: the process where soil is gradually lost through the action of the wind, rain, and ice, as well as human and animal behaviour

sphere of influence: all the things that you can control or affect

sustainable: having the quality of meeting our own needs today and not stopping people in the future from meeting their needs

symptom: a sign, or an indicator, of a bigger problem

tackle: try to deal with a difficult problem or situation

tact: the ability to deal with difficult situations carefully and without doing or saying anything that will annoy or upset other people

tally: a record of the number or amount of something, especially one that you can keep adding to

tally chart: a chart recording the number or amount of something

tend: to care for somebody or something

thrive: to grow or develop well

track: to follow (and often record) the progress or development of somebody/something

underlying: something that is under the surface of, or the reason behind, something else

unintended consequences: results of something that you did not plan to happen

unique: being the only one of its kind

unsustainable: not having the quality of meeting our own needs today and therefore stopping people in the future from meeting their needs

upstream problem: a problem that is the cause of other problems

urban: connected with a town or city

visible: can be seen and noticed

vision: an idea or a picture in your imagination

yield: produce